AUTHENTIC PARENTING

Authentic Parenting

A FOUR-TEMPERAMENTS GUIDE TO UNDERSTANDING YOUR CHILD AND YOURSELF

Bari Borsky ∾ **Judith Haney**

STEINERBOOKS | 2013

STEINERBOOKS
AN IMPRINT OF ANTHROPOSOPHIC PRESS, INC.
610 Main Street, Great Barrington, MA 01230
www.steinerbooks.org

Book design: William Jens Jensen

LIBRARY OF CONGRESS CONTROL NUMBER: 2013950115

ISBN: 978-1-62148-046-4 (paperback)
ISBN: 978-1-62148-047-1 (ebook)

CONTENTS

*This book is dedicated to the memory of
William H. G. Walshe, who woke us up to the fact that
understanding one another is the foundation for building
a community that will endure and thrive.*

ACKNOWLEDGEMENTS

The information that we've gathered about how to work with the four temperaments in children comes primarily from the observations of Waldorf teachers who interact with children in their classroom on a daily basis. A few have written about this subject, and we've referenced them in the bibliography. We would especially like to thank those Waldorf teachers who have not published a book on this topic, but who were willing to take the time to share their knowledge and expertise with us. The insights and wisdom they contributed have allowed us to ground the content of this book in real life experience.

Bari Borsky: It is a pleasure to acknowledge Mimi Devens for the depth of her understanding, enthusiasm, and dedication. As a teacher and a therapist, she works with many children and their parents to facilitate balance, boundaries, consistency, and clarity in the adult/child relationship. I thank her for helping us enrich the content of this book with her experience, professional advice, and thoughtful edits. Bonnie Holden is a very wise and perceptive Waldorf teacher who helped bring the challenges of working with parents' temperaments into focus for me. Mona Lewis is an artistic and insightful Waldorf teacher whose loving attention brings out the best in every one of her students. I am grateful to her for sharing her wisdom on how to work with the different temperaments, and on how they each learn best.

I would like to thank Aurora Winter for challenging me to write a book. Without her encouragement I never would have started this project. I would also like to thank the Highland Hall parents who said they would value having a Four Temperaments Guidebook.

My appreciation goes to Judy Haney for bringing the strengths of her evolved phlegmatic and melancholic temperament to this project. Together we learned much more about the four temperaments, and ourselves, than we ever could have imagined.

Judith Haney: I would like to thank Bari Borsky for decades of enriching friendship, during which we learned from each other how to approach our own and the other's temperaments. Her choleric/sanguine prodded and cajoled my melancholic/phlegmatic to keep moving with this project when my energy lagged.

I would also like to thank Shepha Vainstein, LMFT, for taking time from her busy schedule to share the insights she gained as a phlegmatic parent learning how to best assist her choleric child in the early life stages. And a note of appreciation to Betty Staley for her warm and loving treatment of each temperament in her books. She sees and talks about the best in all of us.

We both are grateful to Jamie Branker, Valerie Spencer, and Babette Zschiegner for being masterful communicators. Valerie, thank you for your perceptive suggestions and eagle eye edits.

ABOUT THE ORGANIZATION OF THIS BOOK

The main body of the book contains four sections, one for each temperament. While the "Introduction" portion for each temperament provides a general overview of that temperament, more specific details appear in the "how to recognize..." and "how to work with..." segments, which focus on the children. The "adult" sections describe three stages of temperament development, as well as indications about how your own temperament may affect children of all four temperaments. The front of the book contains a test for adults to help identify their own dominant and secondary temperaments. This is useful for understanding how one's own temperament may affect children.

About gender: we've chosen to use the "he/she" pronouns in the Introduction to avoid any inference that a given temperament has a given gender. All the temperaments are associated with both male and female and both children and adults. The "he/she" convention used throughout the book, however, would be cumbersome, and as we would like our readers to be able to focus on the attributes being discussed rather than on the gender, we've decided to use the feminine forms for the Sanguine and Melancholic, and the masculine forms for the Choleric and Phlegmatic.

We have referenced our sources of information in the bibliography at the end of this guidebook, and we have cited specific conversations or specific articles as necessary.

INTRODUCTION

"I believe the greatest gift I can conceive of having from anyone is to be seen by them, heard by them. The greatest gift I can give is to see, hear, understand, and to touch another person. When this is done I feel contact has been made." —**Virginia Satir**

We often hear parents say, "My child is my greatest teacher." It is a marvelous and awesome truth that children are mirrors for the parent, challenging them to become better, wiser, and more compassionate human beings. It also means that their children have the ability to identify weakness, insecurity, or lack of experience in the parent, and exploit it to resist authority and have their own way.

Let's face it . . . raising children is not for the faint of heart. We love them to bits, but really . . . how are we to know if our parenting style, discipline program, and way of communicating with our children are effective?

A child's personality is influenced by heredity and environment, elements that are fairly understandable. Then around age six or seven, a powerful internal drive to express their individuality begins to emerge, and the process of individuation can be a challenge for any parent. As our children "change" by growing into their own unique personalities, the once endearing toddler can start to demonstrate "negative" (stubborn, rebellious, flighty, moody) behavior that can make it difficult to see or hear what is going on behind the youngster's resistance. As adults, we respond positively when we are understood by another human being; it gives us permission to trust the other person and to release the need to protect what is most precious to us—our sense of self. Children also respond openly and more trustingly when they feel they have been understood. *Authentic Parenting: A Four-Temperaments Guide to Understanding Your Child—and Yourself!* provides advice and tools for "seeing" deeply into some behavioral characteristics of your child's personality, and tips for working effectively and directly with those aspects.

So what are the four temperaments? The basic elements of personality were first described by Hippocrates (c. 460–370 BC), the father of Western medicine. He identified the fiery and willful choleric; the watery, laidback phlegmatic; the excitable, short-attention-span sanguine; and the hypersensitive, inhibited melancholic. Hippocrates used these "humors," or temperaments, as a way of explaining "imbalance" or illness in his patients.

The theory of temperaments was further observed and evolved by Plato, Aristotle, and Galen, a first-century Roman physician, surgeon, and philosopher. As one of the most accomplished medical researchers of antiquity, Galen contributed greatly to the understanding of numerous scientific disciplines. He was the first to search for psychological reasons in connection with the four temperaments and human behavior.

In eighteenth-century Europe, the "Age of Enlightenment" relegated the theory of the four temperaments to the realm of superstition. Thanks to the work of Sigmund Freud and Carl Jung, new interest in understanding the human psyche and soul blossomed during the nineteenth and twentieth centuries. In 1919, with the creation of the first Waldorf school, Rudolf Steiner, an Austrian scientist and philosopher, instructed teachers in the use of the four temperaments as a tool for unlocking the mystery of each child's personality. He taught them how an understanding of the four temperaments can help to develop harmony within the child. A great deal of what we know today about the four temperaments in children has come from careful observation by teachers in Waldorf schools.

Each one of the temperaments is related to one of the four elements of earth, water, air, and fire. Over the centuries, they have been known by different names—currently they are called *melancholic* (earth), *phlegmatic* (water), *sanguine* (air), and *choleric* (fire). Each temperament has its own basic qualities and attributes, but it has nothing to do with character or morals. Individuals will do things or react in certain ways according to their own temperament, quite irrespective of their upbringing, education, standards, or knowledge.

Every child and adult possesses all four temperaments, but in most cases one or two will predominate. Careful observation will reveal which temperament characteristics the child exhibits and which ones they don't. To be effective, parents will want a "working" understanding of all four temperaments and will guide their child based on the one or two that prominently come to expression. Understanding that childhood itself is a sanguine time of life, we should be mindful that some of these characteristics describe all children.

A child with a dominant *melancholic temperament* experiences inner suffering and senses loss and death more than the other three temperaments do. This is the child whose feelings are always getting hurt, and whose body seems to lack energy. By recognizing and working with the melancholic temperament, parents and teachers can help such children to focus less on themselves and more on those around them by consciously drawing their attention to the pain and struggles of other people or animals. This will help the melancholic child to grow into a compassionate adult who is willing to help alleviate the suffering of others.

Children with *phlegmatic* as the dominant temperament have a tendency to be asleep to the outer world. They prefer to live in a feeling of inner comfort and do not seem to exhibit much interest in things or people around them. These children require special guidance to develop socially acceptable behavior, create friendships, and focus on tasks and projects beyond what is comfortable and easy. With proper attention, these children can grow into adults who find purpose in their ability to research deeply and carefully, and to think profoundly and strategically about any project they take on.

The *sanguine temperament* is social, chatty, and falls in love with every new interest that appears. These children need consistency and guidance in learning how to follow through and finish projects. They require a teacher or mentor who will instill in them the importance of loyalty and keeping one's word. These children can grow into adults who can contribute to the world of fashion, design, the arts, sales, and anything that requires interpersonal relationship skills.

Children who have *choleric* as the dominant temperament are fiery and will-filled. They need adults who know how to work with their blazing energy without suppressing it. These children require someone to teach them how to control themselves, to self-reflect, and to be sensitive to the feelings of other people. Choleric children often grow into visionary business or political leaders whose disciplined will forces are capable of guiding a company of soldiers or a company of business executives.

In today's world, family and school environments are filled with expectations about who we are, or worse, who we "should" be. However, isn't it futile to expect a person who is color blind to see color perfectly, or a person with short legs to become a champion long jumper? In the same way, it is frustrating, demoralizing, and even damaging to a child to expect a melancholic temperament to be outgoing and gregarious, or a sanguine child to sit quietly, focus, and complete every task. Knowledge of the four temperaments can help parents—who are entrusted with the mental, emotional, and physical security of their children—to modify unrealistic expectations. By truly understanding our children and working with what is actually present, we give them our acceptance and the room to grow into the fullness of who they truly are. The result is that "understood" children can grow into adults who are comfortable, effective, authentic, balanced, and accepting of themselves.

As we begin to explore this guidebook for effective parenting, here are a few things to keep in mind:

- Both you and your child demonstrate traits of all four temperaments, but most of the time only one or two will dominate. We feel it is valuable to gain a familiarity with all four temperaments because over time the other less dominant temperaments may appear. For example, human beings are more sanguine during childhood, demonstrate more choleric tendencies during the teenage and young-adult years, and become more phlegmatic in old age. Moreover, understanding of all four temperaments will aid in understanding your child's friends, other family members, business associates, and yourself.

- When only one temperament dominates in the child, the personality will become one-sided. It is the responsibility of parents, teachers, and other close adults to recognize first the character imbalance and then to help children temper or modify their behavior so they can develop and enrich other aspects of their personalities. A child cannot do this without the loving and consistent guidance of an adult. This book is organized so that parents can easily recognize and work with their child's temperament.

- Because temperament colors our perceptions, reactions, and perspective, especially toward our children, we encourage parents to discover their own dominant temperament(s). We have provided a short questionnaire at the beginning of the book that will help the reader do this. There is also a section with brief descriptions on how one's temperament(s) impacts your child and ways to work with your own traits in relation to those of your child.

- Because each of the four temperaments is completely different from the others, as adults we can become impatient and exasperated with one another because of "clashing" personality traits. By making an effort to gain a working understanding of the temperaments and their characteristics, we learn to develop patience and understanding toward ourselves, toward other adults in our life, and, most important, toward our children.

Within each of the four temperaments are strengths that can be used by children who are guided to develop the positive attributes of their nature. An understanding of your child's dominant temperament will aid you in developing communication and discipline techniques that are compassionate and appropriate for your particular child. This understanding will speak directly to your child's personal way of comprehending the world. The gift to your children is that they will feel truly seen and heard. The gift to yourself is a deeper understanding of your child's basic nature and confidence that you have the tools to respond appropriately, effectively, and lovingly.

TEMPERAMENT IDENTIFICATION TEST

Knowing others is wisdom.
Knowing yourself is Enlightenment.
Mastering others is force;
Mastering yourself is Power.

LAO TZU, Chinese Philosopher

Reply to each question with a number from 1 to 6,
1=hardly ever, or I do not agree; and 6=almost always,
or I totally agree.

SECTION 1: YELLOW

1. I consider myself to be an extrovert.   ——

2. I enjoy talking with friends, and sharing
   my experiences with others.   ——

3. I enjoy new and different things.   ——

4. I generally live in the present, because I feel there
   are many interesting things going on in the world.   ——

5. Repetitive routine bores me.   ——

6. I like working with larger concepts and prefer
   to have others work out the details.   ——

7. Spur-of-the-moment activities,
   such as day trips, appeal to me.   ——

8. I enjoy fashion, decorating, or being a host.   ——

9. Surprises do not bother me.   ——

10. I have many interests and move easily
    and often from one to the next.   ——

11. I meet each day with enthusiasm.   ——

12. I enjoy people and their stories.   ——

Add up all the numbers above to get your Yellow Score.   ——

Reply to each question with a number from 1 to 6,
1=hardly ever, or I do not agree; and 6=almost always,
or I totally agree.

SECTION 2: RED

1. I consider myself to be an extrovert. ___

2. Challenges energize me. ___

3. I enjoy competition—in games or at work. ___

4. I generally have my eyes set on the future
   and see many wonderful opportunities. ___

5. I get angry and impatient
   when things don't go the way I want them to. ___

6. I sometimes become angry
   when others tell me what to do. ___

7. I can be impatient
   with incompetent or insecure people. ___

8. I am good in an emergency because
   I am not afraid to take charge. ___

9. I think I am at my best when I am in charge. ___

10. Having achieved my own success,
    I am interested in helping others to do the same. ___

11. I meet each day with great energy. ___

12. I am offended when things aren't fair. ___

Add up all the numbers above to get your Red Score. ___

Reply to each question with a number from 1 to 6,
1=hardly ever, or I do not agree; and 6=almost always,
or I totally agree.

SECTION 3: BLUE

1. I consider myself to be an introvert. ___

2. I often find life's responsibilities overwhelming. ___

3. Physical activity takes considerable effort on my part. ___

4. I often dwell on the past. ___

5. I take life very seriously. ___

6. I see the sad and gloomy side of life. ___

7. It is wise to prepare for disasters
   instead of just "hoping for the best." ___

8. I find volunteer work to be fulfilling. ___

9. I often feel very lonely. ___

10. Reading stories of others overcoming difficulties
    fills me with sympathy for their suffering. ___

11. It takes a real effort to get moving in the morning. ___

12. I usually don't notice that someone else is
    suffering unless it is pointed out to me. ___

Add up all the numbers above to get your Blue Score. ___

Reply to each question with a number from 1 to 6,
1=hardly ever, or I do not agree; and 6=almost always,
or I totally agree.

SECTION 4: GREEN

1. I consider myself to be an introvert. ____

2. I am uncomfortable in competitive situations. ____

3. Change is easier for me to accept
    when approached gradually. ____

4. My mind is on the present and on my inner comfort. ____

5. I prefer a steady routine with no interruptions. ____

6. I don't react very well to surprises. ____

7. I need detailed instructions to complete
    a new task successfully. ____

8. I will stick to a task until it is completed
    to the last detail. ____

9. I am generally content to be left to myself. ____

10. I become interested in new subjects by hearing
    about, and sharing, my friends' interests. ____

11. I enjoy waking slowly and reliving my dreams
    before facing the noisy outside world. ____

12. I am faithful and loyal to my friends. ____

Add up all the numbers above to get your Green Score. ____

FINAL SCORE

Enter all four scores below. The highest one indicates the predominating temperament. If two are high, then two predominate. If all are about the same, your temperaments are well balanced.

SANGUINE (YELLOW)   ____

CHOLERIC (RED)   ____

MELANCHOLIC (BLUE)   ____

PHLEGMATIC (GREEN)   ____

NOTES

SANGUINE: THE RAINBOW BUTTERFLY

The ice-cold stream comes bubbling down the mountain,
Churning around the fallen log, jumping over rocks,
Twisting here and turning there,
Careless of its final destination.
Cheerfully it helps maintain the meadow's teeming life,
Refreshing, cleansing all along its route.
Heedless of the future summer's drought,
It merrily passes by, and is gone.

—Judith Haney

If we were to choose an image that symbolizes the essence of the sanguine temperament, it would be the butterfly—a delicate creature that flits from flower to flower, dancing on the wind and enchanting us with its ethereal lightness and beauty. On the other hand, your sanguine child might be a bit earthier and resemble the character of Roo in Winnie the Pooh stories, bouncing from one thing to another with a liveliness that is hard to contain.

The sanguine child has many interests and none of them will last very long. She can bless a new project or a new friend with her infectious enthusiasm, and then without warning lose interest and leave the project or friend, without a backward glance. Just as the butterfly moves from flower to flower across the landscape, the sanguine moves from one interest to another, never lingering very long.

The sanguine temperament has a relationship to the air. This child can seem light as a summer breeze, or she can be as rough as a tornado. These children are extraverted and love social inter-action. They hang on other children like clothes, wanting to be close, involved, and engaged. They are often found in the middle of groups of children, talking, talking, talking. They live in the moment and love to share in everything that is happening. They are filled with tidbits of information, mostly superficial and often incorrect. They are prone to gossip, because this is a way to express their love of social engagement. Because they desire to taste, touch, and experience each new thing that draws their attention, the san-guine child's life is never boring, and each new phenomenon is greeted with wonder and acceptance.

The challenge for parents of a sanguine is learning techniques to help your child complete a project, delve deeper into a subject (or into her own feelings and motivations), and to be conscious that other people (children) are hurt when she suddenly loses interest in the friendship. If they haven't learned to temper their tendency toward superficiality and fleeting interest at a young age, teenage and adult sanguines can get a reputation for being fickle.

Because they are so easily distracted by new stimuli—be it situations, school subjects, or people, there is a danger that these children could be misdiagnosed as having the distracted type of ADHD, when in fact they are just expressing their personality through the sanguine temperament.

Physically, sanguines are generally attractive, with a physique that is not too skinny and not too fat. Their walk is light and airy, and their faces are bright and intelligent. The physical expression lies in the nervous system, so these children will be supple and slender with facial features that are mobile, expressive, and changeable.

HOW TO RECOGNIZE THE SANGUINE TEMPERAMENT

SANGUINE CHILDREN EXPRESS A LOVE OF LIFE

Unlike melancholic or phlegmatic children who tend toward introspection, sanguine children are extraverts and give expression to this through a love of social engagement. They like to be in the middle of everything that is happening, and they are especially enthusiastic about the new and fresh, such as friends, clothes, and games. Life for the sanguine is always an adventure, rarely boring, and because they are fun to be with, they are seldom alone.

- Sanguine children, both girls and boys, are chatterboxes. They love to talk and demonstrate an ability to speak expressively and fluently. However, as they get caught up in their verbal tale, they often fail to come to the point. Most sanguines are overflowing with information that they want to share, but unless there is also a strong phlegmatic tendency, the knowledge can be superficial and the facts incorrect.
- There is a restless energy in this temperament that makes her appear to be in constant motion. She enjoys being on the go, engaging in numerous activities (sometimes all at once), and surrounding herself with friends. What she may not enjoy is holding still long enough to do something serious like homework.
- The sanguine child really lives "in the moment" and has no interest in the past. Her mistakes are of little concern to her, and when she gets into disagreements or fights, she won't stay angry for long or carry a grudge. Unlike the melancholic or phlegmatic, the sanguine temperament tends not to reflect on her feelings or actions.

- If this temperament is very one-sided, your child can be quite dreamy.

MOODINESS IS A TRAIT

- Sanguine children are quite open and loving, and can easily reach out to others with light-hearted warmth and affection. They can also turn into a hurricane of emotions if something upsets them.
- This temperament is associated with the nervous system, so emotional ups and downs are the fabric of this child's life. She can be ecstatically engaged, interested, and involved one moment and unable to cope in another. Her nervous system can't really manage too much overstimulation.
- Because she is interested in so many things, she can easily become overcommitted, which can lead the child to be over-stressed and have frequent "melt downs." Her sanguine nature causes her to quickly pick up a new project, and just as quickly drop it and never pick it up again.

THE CHALLENGE OF ESTABLISHING GOOD HABITS

In his book *Understanding Our Fellow Men*, Knud Asbjorn Lund makes the point that it is because the sanguine temperament moves from one activity to the next so quickly that her interest tends to be superficial, and she appears to be fickle. If the sanguine child also exhibits strong phlegmatic traits, it will mitigate the superficial tendencies of the sanguine nature. Because it is difficult for the sanguine child to "pay attention" to any one subject for very long, without guidance and support from an adult, her education will tend to have holes in it. This child seems very bright because she is able to pick up ideas rapidly, but once her attention wanes, the ideas are quite forgotten.

- What can be frustrating for parents and teachers is the sanguine's lack of persistence. Completing homework assignments or chores is a challenge because it is in the nature of this "air being" to become easily bored or distracted. These children can easily become impatient and forgetful; consequently, they won't stay with a task or project long enough to complete it or to gain meaningful experience.

- Like the choleric, sanguine children are more interested in what is going on around them, rather than inside them. However, unlike the choleric, they don't have a driving impulse to accomplish something. The sanguine is focused on enjoying the immediate present and doesn't worry about the future.

- Because she delights in everything new, the sanguine is likely to drop friends as easily as she makes them. Adults can work with this tendency to keep her from becoming fickle.

THE NERVOUS SYSTEM DOMINATES

This child (and adult) lives strongly in her senses. The challenge is that her interest can become disinterest very quickly because some other new enchantment has grabbed her attention.

- Sanguines become fascinated in everything outside of themselves and don't have a natural ability to self-reflect. An important task for the parent is to help the sanguine child learn this skill. Without it, she grows into an adult without an internal compass. Continually teaching the child how to "circle back" to a previously dropped task will build good habits for the future.

- New impressions easily arouse the imagination, but then even newer ones wipe out the old ones leaving little or no memory or impact. Assisting your child to "review" the day will help her build up an ability to "remember."

- Parents and teachers should keep in mind that this child becomes bored easily when it seems like nothing is happening. Her nervous system keeps demanding new stimulation.

- The strong relationship to the nervous system causes these children to seem like they are in perpetual movement; they run up and down stairs instead of walking, or they continually get up from the desk for water, food, or a bathroom break. These are the students that can't sit still in their chairs and tend to put their feet up on the desk.

DISCERNMENT AND RULES

Sanguine children can cause frustration and alarm because they refuse to be put in a box, and for them, rules exist to be broken...not maliciously, but certainly mischievously.

- According to Lund, it is difficult for this temperament to draw a line between truth and lies, reality and fantasy, reliability and unreliability. This child sees goodness in the world and is easily duped.

- She tends to be a great storyteller and exaggerates freely. However, when her exaggeration (or lie) is pointed out to her, she will make light of it and won't give it a second thought. If she feels she is being pressured into doing something she doesn't want to do, she won't hesitate to fabricate a story or tell a lie.

- This disregard for the rules can alarm parents when suddenly the child dashes across the street without regard to traffic or regulations, then just as suddenly dashes back again, smiling mischievously, causing your heart to miss a beat.

A Love of Life

- Things come easily to the sanguine. She plays piano by ear, paints passably without any knowledge of color or technique, and is good at games without ever having learned the rules.
- Unlike the melancholic child, the sanguine is able to bounce back from minor physical ailments. An illness that keeps her from socializing with her friends and away from the excitement of life is of no interest to her.
- The sanguine takes in the world through her senses, so she enjoys eating. Trying new foods is an adventure, especially when the occasion is social. She tends to eat small quantities (these children are likely to be thin), and if the food is delicious, she will often rapturously compliment the cook.
- Unless she has been over-stimulated by the day's impressions, your child will drop off to sleep easily without any problem.
- Sanguine children love to live in their imagination, and with their innate sense of design and love of style, these youngsters enjoy choosing clothes that match their image. She might choose to be a ballet dancer one week, a queen the next. He might be inspired to dress like a soldier or a rock musician. They will live in the fantasy of that personality for a while. Older sanguine children (and adults) will become particular about wanting to dress in the latest style, or a style that reflects their unique personality.
- According to Betty Staley, author of *Between Form and Freedom, A Practical Guide for the Teenage Years*, the word "love" is associated with the sanguine. These children bring a love of life, a sense of adventure, and delightful enthusiasm

to the family. The chaos that surrounds this child is good-natured, fun-filled, and light-hearted.

HOW TO WORK WITH THE SANGUINE CHILD

Parents are advised to step lightly with the sanguine; the innocence of life is one of the key qualities the adult needs to keep in mind. The sanguine child is a delight and a worry, but she is also a symbol of eternal childhood in the human soul.

CHARACTER DEVELOPMENT

Learning to Complete Tasks and Stay Centered

This child thrives on change. She is interested in everything and anything and has a difficult time holding her attention on any one subject or friendship for very long. It is this behavioral characteristic that can resemble ADHD. In guiding the sanguine child, great emphasis will need to be placed on completing a task, developing lasting interests, and strengthening the will.

Encourage Rhythmical Tasks

It is helpful if the task is rhythmical because the sanguine will learn to anticipate the task, and this helps her stay centered. Setting the table, emptying the garbage, folding towels, and checking the mailbox are repeatable chores that work well. If the task can include elements of beauty, such as setting the table or helping arrange flowers, so much the better. According to Mimi Devens—therapist, Waldorf class teacher, and mother of two daughters—parents of a sanguine would be wise not to "yell out" tasks, or list two or three things to be done at once because this child will unlikely be successful at remembering them. Stay close and be consistent, as she can easily become distracted. It would be most effective if you remain nearby and offer reminders and redirection, for it is the sanguine's nature to become distracted and float away.

Keep the sanguine focused on the process of a task (paying attention to details) rather than just the end result. Over a period of time, more and more emphasis should be placed on doing a job well. This child wants your approval, so be sure to acknowledge when she notices things she wouldn't normally notice, or when there is improvement or success.

In a conversation with Mona Lewis, Waldorf handwork teacher and mother of a sanguine daughter, she observed that if you admire her gifts (sense of color, ability to make things beautiful, graceful dance movements), it helps the child become present to the depths of things.

Provide Interests That Require a Short Attention Span

According to Rudolf Steiner, the founder of Waldorf education, providing many things that require only fleeting interest may instill a desire in the child to stay longer with something, and gradually the child's attention span will improve. Drawing, puzzles, board games, quick knitting or crochet projects, and baking cookies are some examples.

The sanguine child compensates for her short attention span by quickly picking up anything to which she gives her attention, but it is just as quickly forgotten. Mimi Devens advises parents not to go out and buy some expensive musical instrument just because she is wildly enthusiastic to learn to play it. Be a little patient and wait. The passion that she exhibits today may well pass. As a parent your task will be to help her to stick with something somewhere along the way. Little bits of information repeated often help the sanguine child to learn and to become more grounded.

Be Prepared to Make Many Topics of Interest Available

Provide many different topics of interest until one appears to be more important. Then find various ways to support that one so that it grows as an interest for the child. Rudolf Steiner has suggested that teachers keep the child busy at regular intervals with subjects that warrant only a passing interest so she can be justifiably sanguine about them. Then remove them so the child desires them again. Then bring them back into the child's sphere of activity again. As the sanguine becomes engaged in a subject or activity this way, a small miracle happens: she permits herself to be captured by serious subjects. Parents working with the child in this way need to be conscious, deliberate, methodical, and consistent if they want this technique to be successful.

Limit Overstimulation

Studies have shown that television, computer and computer games, and electronic devices over-stimulate a child's brain receptors and increase the risk of ADHD-type symptoms or characteristics. The sanguine child lives strongly in her nervous system and is prone to distractibility, a short attention span, and flighty behavior. Limiting or eliminating television and electronic devices while the child's brain is still developing is highly recommended.

DISCIPLINING THE SANGUINE CHILD

Reflect Back the Consequences of Their Behavior

Sanguine children especially want to love and be loved, but their airy, sylphlike nature can be a source of frustration to friends, family, and teachers. Parents can gently reflect back to the sanguine the consequences of her behavior. Repetition and rhythm are extremely important when working with the sanguine temperament: repeat instructions and use the same words. Work with your child so she learns to follow through. The sanguine is going to want love, but friends won't be there if her fickle behavior hurts them. Parents can provide boundaries that are somewhat flexible and transparent that won't damage her "light-hearted" nature, but will help her understand that there are limitations and consequences. Remember that the sanguine child doesn't self-reflect, so she counts on her parents to help her be aware.

Act Immediately When There Is an Incident

When a choleric child misbehaves, it is best to wait until the child cools down before reviewing the incident. The sanguine child is the exact opposite. Parents and teachers must act immediately when there has been an incident because the sanguine child does not have an interest in past problems. She quickly forgets all transgressions—her own and those of others.

The Importance of an Authority Figure

It is important that this child respects her parents. It is far more beneficial for the child if she regards her parents as authority figures rather than as friends. It is important to say what you mean, and mean what you say. Set boundaries and stick to them. Your sanguine child often lacks discernment, so parents who are authority figures can help the child to feel safe by setting boundaries. Don't try to win your child's approval by giving her too many choices.

Scolding and Punishment Are Not Effective

It is not unusual for parents to have their patience taxed regarding discipline, because scolding and punishment have a limited effect on the sanguine. Unlike the choleric child who will fight excessive discipline, trying to dominate a sanguine child could lead her to become extremely superficial. Her reaction will be to lie, or make light of serious offenses. However, she does want to please her parents or teachers, so loving and consistent presence, reminders, and guidance can go a long way.

Work with, Not against, this Temperament

Even though parents may find this temperament trying, it is wisest to "work with it," not against it. It is not possible to "change" the sanguine, or to control her. To do so is to invite subterfuge and deception. This child will tell lies if an authority figure tries to dominate her. Parents should strive to be the consistent, loving authority, always guiding and redirecting. The sanguine wants to please, so, like a sheepdog, be sure to bring her back within boundaries when her behavior has gone too far astray. Rhythms, like regular mealtimes or bedtime, for the sanguine, as with all children, are healing and soothing.

Cultivate Compassion

Warmth and encouragement are necessary for the child's continued development. Don't lose your temper or the child will lose respect for you. It is okay to teach her about how frustrated other people are with her behavior, but do so with kindness and encouragement.

LOVE AND ATTACHMENT HELP DEVELOP LONG-LASTING INTEREST

The Importance of Love for One Person

Even though the sanguine is ever so fickle, it is important for this child to find one adult for whom there will be a continuous and permanent significance. Rudolf Steiner emphasized to teachers that it is only by the indirect way of love for one person that interest in that person will be developed. It is the responsibility of the parents or teacher to foster in the sanguine child a love for one person, and if successful, this love can cure one-sidedness in the temperament.

The phlegmatic child learns by imitating adult behavior. The melancholic child learns by developing sympathy for the pain of others and understanding how they have overcome hardship. The choleric child learns best when he feels respect for an authority figure. The sanguine child will learn from an adult with whom she can develop personal love and from whom she receives love.

The Effect of Kindness and Compliments

It cannot be emphasized enough that the sanguine wants to please. Just as they learn when they receive continuous small bites of information, it also supports them to know when their actions gratify their parents or teacher. Share with the sanguine how much something pleases you, and she will find a way to bring you happiness. Also, even if she frustrates you, treat the sanguine with kindness. She respects those adults who see through her idiosyncrasies, but she loses respect for adults who become angry and lose their self-control.

> *While doing grief recovery coaching, one of my clients, who spent a lifetime being her own strict taskmaster so as never to disappoint anyone, felt there was very little happiness in her life. "I'm really a very social person. I really do like people and I really do like to have fun." She sought coaching support because a serious loss had left her life joyless. What I heard was a sanguine temperament that had never been given permission to be authentic. Even though she tried, as a child she could not please her parents, and rarely received a compliment from any adult. As I was in the process of completing this book about the four temperaments, I asked my client if I could read the "Sanguine Introduction" page to her. After I finished reading, she exclaimed, "Oh my, that's me!" Then, between her tears she whispered, "I feel like I've been seen for the first time in my life."*

ENVIRONMENT

The Importance of a Calm Environment

Parents should pay particular attention to the home environment, especially the sanguine child's bedroom. Prints are stimulating, so solid colors would be preferable for their calming effect. Warm yellows and oranges will bring sunshine into the environment. When the room is simple, it will allow her nervous system to rest. When there is order and beauty in her environment, your child can relax.

Display Her Many Interests

The sanguine child's room should be kept simple. Because she will have many interests, shelves to display her collections are advised. Boxes, large baskets, and utility drawers to keep toys and stuffed animals in will help contain the chaos. Your child can relax in a beautiful, tidy environment, and if you are willing to help her clean her room, harmony can be achieved and maintained.

Make Chores Fun and Magical

Life is a game for this child, and much can be learned if the parent can maintain a sense of magic and fun in doing chores. Have the bedroom become a cave and the floor has to be kept clear for the dragon, or it is a beautiful palace being prepared for a dance. Stay close at hand and know that you may have to offer many reminders about keeping her room clean, or doing her chores.

> *One parent said that she always helped her child clean her room. It was their together time, and the shared activity helped to build fairly stress-free good habits in the child.*

Help Your Child Overcome Egoism

The sanguine temperament has less will power to rise above her egoism than the other temperaments. If parents can lovingly reflect back that her fickle behavior will cost her friends, or remind her that other children won't want to play with someone who is so changeable, this will help support her desire to overcome selfishness. Remember, the sanguine wants to please. When reality crashes into her sense of self, like children not wanting to be friends with her, she will feel small and give in. It is in this moment that she can change her attitude and allow herself to be influenced. Wonderful qualities can be brought out if the sanguine is treated with a gentle but determined hand.

THE SANGUINE ADULT

DEVELOPING EFFECTIVE RELATIONSHIPS

"You must do the thing you think you cannot do."
—Eleanor Roosevelt

THE THREE STAGES OF THE ADULT SANGUINE TEMPERAMENT

The first-stage sanguine adult could be described as social, chatty, imaginative, nervous, and extremely variable. The thinking can be swift and fleeting because the sanguine tries to think about many things at once and this makes it difficult for her to hold her focus. She shows an interest in anything new and different, but the interest does not penetrate deeply. Before there is time to get to know a subject or new friend well, the sanguine has moved on to the next thing that captures her attention. It takes inner will and some time for ideas, impressions, and imaginations to be transformed into experience, but the first-stage sanguine doesn't intuitively reflect, and therefore lacks the necessary inner resources and endurance when confronted with life's challenges. She doesn't take responsibility for her "commitments," and will leave friends or associates to deal with the consequences for the things she starts but doesn't complete. The sanguine child and first-stage adult start many projects, but seldom complete any of them.

The second-stage sanguine begins to realize how much she needs focus. She has good intentions for herself and her children, but at this stage challenges still rattle her and she lacks the strength of character to follow through. She wants to be a great parent because she knows her child needs her, but whenever she meets obstacles, she turns the focus back on herself. When the sanguine overcomes the temptation to give up, run away, or ignore obstacles and challenges, she will have begun to transform her sanguinity.

The third-stage sanguine is much less self-centered, and far more focused. She is still intuitive, but now she has life experience and depth that help her understand others. She takes pleasure in using her life experience to assist others, and no longer requires recognition. She is still optimistic, enjoys relationships, and can take the time to feel gratitude for what life brings her.

THE SANGUINE PARENT

What could be more fun than a parent who is interested in everything, delights in doing things on the spur of the moment, and loves to play? But when the spur-of-the-moment or unstructured routine or changes in direction become the norm, the children suffer.

The sanguine parent's first responsibility is to strengthen her sense of self and focus on the needs of the children. By making a commitment to be a conscientious and responsible adult, the sanguine can minimize the fleeting perceptions, images, feelings, and sensations that are characteristic of this temperament. Doing so will create greater order and routine, and minimize the chaos for the children.

- If your child has a *phlegmatic temperament,* your sanguinity and changeability could be torture. All children need routine—regular meal times and regular bedtime. For the phlegmatic child, routine is essential and without it the child will likely feel stressed. He may throw tantrums or fall apart. When we do not recognize and work with the temperament a child has come into this world with, we diminish their potential. Every child's temperament is an inherent quality that can't be changed. A parent that is not conscious of her own sanguinity may fail to recognize the phlegmatic child's need for a "regular" schedule, habits, and ritual.

- A sanguine parent who thoughtlessly or unwittingly changes the routine, or has no routine at all, will have a phlegmatic child with digestive problems. The phlegmatic temperament lives in the metabolism, so it might be helpful to use the cow as an analogy. If he doesn't want sick animals, the farmer is careful to feed and milk his herd on a schedule. The farmer must adjust to the needs of the cow and not vice versa, because a cow, by nature, is unable to adjust to sudden changes in routine. So it is with the phlegmatic child.

- Mimi Devens, therapist and Waldorf teacher, has observed that for the sanguine parent, who barely needs to eat, waiting for the phlegmatic to unfold the place mat, get everything as it *should* be, methodically set out his place and food, and begin to eat one course at a time is maddening. Your phlegmatic child is your teacher, reminding you of your own need for rhythm, good habits, and patience.

- The sanguine parent who continually changes her mind or doesn't remember her promises will cause her *choleric* child to lose respect for her. It is a challenge for the sanguine adult to say what she means and mean what she says, but this is exactly what is necessary in raising a choleric child; otherwise the child will run roughshod over the parents and the household. While the choleric child is quite capable, no child ought to be in charge. Too much sanguine chaos and unpredictability creates an inordinate amount of stress for the choleric who needs things well managed.

- Being introverted and extremely serious, the *melancholic* child will feel unseen and not understood by the sanguine adult who tries to jolly the child out of her somber mood, or mocks her for her "sour" attitude.

- It is difficult for any parent to understand the suffering of the melancholic child, but it is particularly challenging for the light-hearted sanguine temperament. A sanguine is not inclined to hold onto feelings, especially pain, for that long. The melancholic child, who lives in her suffering and needs compassion, will not feel she is taken seriously by a sanguine adult who is unable to validate her feelings. The melancholic child does not need an undue amount of sympathy as much as she needs her feelings acknowledged. Listening language such as "I can understand how you could feel that way," or "I remember feeling that way myself," acknowledges the child without trying to make things better or right. Sometimes the melancholic child needs her perceptions challenged. "It sounds like you had a bad moment on the playground, but *not the whole day*." The goal is to help the melancholic child develop the skills to make a reasonable appraisal of her experience.

- The sanguine parent will need to "slow down" when working with children who are *melancholic* or *phlegmatic* because these children need time... to shop, to do homework, to tell a story.

The challenge for the sanguine parent: Learn how to take a breath and give your child the greatest gift of all—your attention. Staying focused on the child's need for rhythm and stability allows the sanguine parent to move into higher stages of her temperament. The sanguine is the temperament of childhood—fun loving, light hearted, and changeable. These delightful characteristics keep the sanguine "youthful" throughout her whole life. The challenge for the sanguine parent is to be fun loving, but also to be the responsible, focused, and centered adult for the children.

CHOLERIC: THE WARRIOR/HERO

The desert flood comes out of nowhere,
Crashing down the mountainside in a dynamic torrent,
Rejoicing in the exhilarating fall,
Hurrying on with impatience to its appointed end,
Perishing in confusion and anger beneath the desert floor.

Its goal was to join the ocean,
To experience the power surging in its depths.
With indifference it pushed aside all obstacles,
Destroying all that blocked its way,
And reached not its desired goal, but oblivion.

—Judith Haney

It's not too difficult to spot the choleric child on the playground. He is the one in the middle of a group of youngsters organizing the other children into a game. He will be shouting instructions while running out the classroom door and gulping down a snack all at the same time. The choleric child is a whirlwind of compact energy with a dynamic disposition. The element associated with this temperament is fire.

Like cholerics Napoleon Bonaparte, General George Patton, and Hilary Clinton, this child believes he can do anything. The choleric child (and adult) delights in breaking down obstacles, even when others have found a situation impossible, because a choleric believes in his own abilities. Of course, what this means to parents is that this child can be stubborn and argumentative.

Those with a dominant choleric temperament are natural born leaders. They have no problem taking charge of a situation, and they have a mind of their own from a very early age. These children and adults have high ideals, and they are prepared to sacrifice to reach their goals. This is a child that will know what it wants to do in life, and parents will often feel like they have little influence.

Cholerics need followers, so in the Winnie the Pooh stories, Rabbit is the choleric character who leads the other animals into situations and adventures. A child with this temperament is an extravert, and his fiery temperament often manifests as anger and impatience. Unless she is a choleric herself, it can be a difficult temperament for a teacher to handle. In order for the choleric child to develop his natural leadership qualities, parents must be willing to guide and discipline his passionate energy. Even at an early age this temperament shows plainly that he dislikes being "ordered about" or giving in to other people, so knowing how to work with him is essential.

This personality loves competitive games and has the physical stamina to be good at strenuous sports. Choleric children are self-directed, and you can identify them by their firm walk that pounds the earth. Typically, their bodies are short and compact, and their gestures are assertive, confident, and purposeful. Their voices are strong, often blustery, and they easily command a room with their presence.

Within this temperament there is great potential to change the world. Choleric adults can become capable, dynamic, and effective leaders with a heightened sense of their own abilities. They are fearless, have high ideals, and were once challenging children that parents and teachers recognized and loved enough to help develop their potential.

HOW TO RECOGNIZE THE CHOLERIC TEMPERAMENT

THE CHOLERIC HAS A STRONG SENSE OF HIS OWN INDIVIDUALITY

Despite the common stamp of their temperament, choleric children vary from one another more than any other temperament. This is because cholerics have such a strong sense of their own individuality that they do not want to be like anyone else. They experience their own uniqueness, and they want to express the characteristics of their own personalities in everything they do. Choleric children are tightly wound, frequently explosive, fearless bundles of energy, facing the world with boldness and a will that wants to dominate.

- This temperament, with its strong ego force, feels that it was born to rule. They are masters of their own bodies and minds, and can quickly become frustrated when their bodies don't respond to their will (*i.e.* when they become ill, or when they fumble while learning a sport or musical instrument). The choleric can become obsessively determined to overcome anything that stands between his will and his goal.

- The choleric child sets high ideals for himself and doesn't hesitate to make sacrifices in order to achieve his objective.

- As a social being, the sanguine child wants to be part of anything that is happening. The choleric child (and adult) is different in that he needs followers, so he will assert himself in all circumstances. He believes his mastery extends to playmates and adults as well. His overwhelming need to be the leader can seem like "bullying" to other children.

- This personality thrives on challenges and takes delight in overcoming obstacles. Even when others have found a situation to be impossible, cholerics so believe in their own abilities that, against all odds, they will still try to achieve the unachievable. The slogan of the U.S. Armed Forces expresses the choleric attitude perfectly: "The difficult we do immediately; the impossible takes a little longer."

- The choleric never wants to show that he is afraid, so he will cover up fear through activity. He will throw himself into the task at hand, using activity to mask insecurity or worry. He always wants to appear tough and self-reliant.

- This temperament refuses to look at the facts of the situation clearly and objectively. Because he believes he can "muscle" his way through any situation, parents and teachers will need to help the choleric learn how to think about outcomes before acting.

- It isn't difficult to identify the choleric child in a room full of children. His voice is strong, he has a tendency to shout, his personality is big, and his presence is powerful.

INSENSITIVITY TO OTHER PEOPLE'S FEELINGS

- A sense of self is important to this child, so he can be oblivious to the feelings of others. He demands a great deal from himself and lives strongly in the ideal; consequently he will have little patience with other children (and adults) who are weak. This temperament is always looking toward the future and doesn't reflect back to the times when he was ill; therefore he doesn't develop patience or empathy for others who are sick.

- One negative aspect of the uncultivated and undeveloped choleric is that he tends to be domineering, intolerant, obstinate, and often blind to consequences. This child can become bossy with people who stand in his way. An argument between two cholerics (male or female) can seem like two male animals fighting for dominance; it is an aggressive and loud experience.

- These children are generally clever, possess a rigid code of honor, and they have contempt for those who break promises or show weakness in the face of difficulties. A key characteristic of the choleric temperament is that he can become very angry and smolder for a long time when something isn't fair or just, or he feels he has been treated unfairly.

An attorney friend tells the story that his parents promised a reward if he achieved superior grades in middle school. Being choleric he accepted the challenge and earned the outstanding grades, but the reward never materialized. Today he is over fifty years old, but he is still deeply offended that his parents didn't keep their word, because he feels he was treated unfairly.

It is worth noting that this same choleric attorney feels satisfied with his career when "justice has been done."

In her book *Between Form and Freedom: A Practical Guide for the Teenage Years,* Betty Staley writes that, if the choleric's honor is attacked, he can be vicious, seeing himself defending "the right and just" while battling to the death.

The choleric loves a challenge and is always charging ahead to realize his perceived immediate or long-term goal, oblivious of the fact that he might be doing so at the expense of other people's feelings. He won't hesitate to take over other children's toys, push his way to the front of the line to play tetherball, or rudely exclude children from playing on "his" team if they aren't athletic enough.

The Challenge for Parents and Teachers

- While still quite young, the choleric shows plainly that he has a mind of his own and dislikes giving in to other people. The choleric child will know what he wants to do in life, and parents will have little influence once the child has made up his mind.

- A teacher without an understanding of the four temperaments could perceive the choleric as a "problem child." In his wonderful article in *Renewal* magazine about the choleric temperament, Thomas Poplawski observes that this child can be easily, and possibly unfairly, labeled as a bully. Often the choleric is just being his overbearing self and slowly learning to interact harmoniously with others.

- It is essential to realize that no choleric can stand criticism. Ironically, the more deeply egoistic the nature, the more sensitive they are to criticism. These children (and adults) find it difficult to apologize, and even though they might not give it, they very much want to be met with respect.

- They experience themselves by "doing" things and may be out of touch with their own feelings and thoughts. Parents and teachers need to keep this in mind when these children "act out."

- The choleric child can be a source of frustration for adults because he seems to challenge everything they say. He is so confident in himself that he feels that he has to have something to say about every subject, regardless of his familiarity with the topic at hand.

STRONG BODY GESTURES

- One can recognize the choleric temperament in a child by the dynamic forcefulness of his gestures, which can be dramatic, assertive, and purposeful. When he loses his temper, his whole body expresses his outrage, including raised fists and arms that want to lash out at something.

- There is determination in his walk as his heels dig into the earth with each step. One receives the impression from his firm walk that he is pounding the ground.
- Choleric children appear to pace because they are always poised for action. If inactive for too long, this temperament will fill the classroom (or the car or home) with tension and restlessness until he can be "uncaged," or until his will is engaged.
- He can be a bull in a china shop. Even though he tries to be careful, the determination that fills his whole physicality causes him to bump into things, knock stuff over, or push into people.

THE CHOLERIC AT SCHOOL

- A choleric student can quickly destroy harmony in the class if he can't find a healthy outlet for his bountiful energy. However, if his energy is given a constructive place to flow, he can help move the entire class forward. Choleric children like to see results, and they learn by overcoming challenges and excelling.
- These children usually enjoy school. They are happy to do the work that needs to be done, they love to be challenged physically and intellectually, and they enjoy helping the teacher with tasks.
- He has an inventive mind and doesn't mind hard work. He can carry out a task quickly and efficiently and doesn't usually require, or desire, supervision.
- When putting on a class play, the choleric child can remind us of the character Bottom, the overconfident weaver chosen to play Pyramus, in Shakespeare's *Midsummer's Night Dream*. This child will quickly learn his role in the play, and then rapidly learn everyone else's part. The teacher will have no

problem getting him to speak out strongly, and he will be the one to hold the play together. Because they are leaders and like to show other children how to do something, they become the self-appointed directors.

- He is good at competitive games and will excel at any strenuous sport that requires physical stamina.

- Because of his energy, initiative, and taste for adventure, the choleric can often be found at the center of whatever is happening. As a natural organizer he attracts followers, and even though he will rarely consult with other children in deciding what to do, he is perceived as a respected and popular leader by the other students.

- The choleric child is sociable enough to charm others, including the teacher.

HOW TO WORK WITH THE CHOLERIC CHILD

It is just as delightful to meet an adult choleric who has overcome his egoism as it is unpleasant to deal with a still egoistical and undisciplined choleric child. Knud Asbjorn Lund describes the mature adult choleric this way: "The choleric adult becomes the fatherly friend who may be completely trusted. He is a pillar of strength in adversity, and is ever resourceful. People seek and respect his judgment for they know he is always right. He is inwardly sure of himself and never demands appreciation."

GUIDANCE AND COMMUNICATION

Do Not Try to "Break" the Choleric Nature

The choleric temperament is energetic and highly extraverted and can be quite a handful for any parent or teacher who isn't choleric. Even as young children, cholerics know their own mind, want their own way, and can be quarrelsome and obstinate. They come off as too self-assured and too bossy. It is very tempting for an adult to try to break the child's belligerent and aggressive behavior. However, this would be in vain. Trying to break a choleric child creates a pattern of resentment that can last into adulthood. It would be better to win this child's heart by gaining his respect, by being mindful that he wants to be competent and excellent, and remembering that he is very proud and sensitive to fairness and justice.

According to Waldorf teacher Bonnie Holden, one effective technique is to offer the choleric a challenge: "Let's see how many toys you can pick up in seven minutes." Challenge him to do a specific task for a specific amount of time, and be sure to acknowledge him if he succeeds. Choleric children want an opportunity to be heroic and they love praise. If you promise a reward for his success, make sure you keep your word and give him the reward.

Clear and Direct Communication without Ambiguity

The adults need to be clear and direct in communicating to their child what they want of him, when they want it, and how they want it. Whereas the melancholic child lives deep within herself, the choleric child lives at the outer edges of his personality. According to Poplawski's article in *Renewal* magazine, subtle hints about proper and improper behavior and wishful thoughts that the young choleric will change his ways will not work. One must be prepared to look the choleric child in the eye and lay down the law. Clarity and directness are what this child requires and respects.

Saving Face

When confronting the choleric, it is important to allow him to save face. If the child has a temper tantrum or is overly aggressive, it would be best not to approach him while he is still "hot." Let the fire and anger simmer down before talking to him, and then go over the incident step by step, quietly and objectively. Parents can guide him to experience for himself what happened and what role his behavior played. Use words like "I didn't think it was fair when you did that." It is very painful for the choleric to realize he was wrong, and an apology won't happen without encouragement. As children, they may not yet *want* to do the right thing or make amends, but part of their moral development will be to learn that being right comes from doing right. Deep in his heart the choleric wants to be respectful and to be respected, so helping him become a leader with integrity ultimately helps him step into his correct role in his class, and eventually in the world.

Help the Child to Self-Reflect

Whereas the melancholic child is thin-skinned, the choleric is thick-skinned and not very sensitive to his surroundings. It is the parent's job to help him learn to self-reflect. Asking him what he thinks of his own conduct, such as, "Did you think your behavior was up to your own standards," or "Do you think you were being fair," is helpful. If the choleric child's behavior breeds disrespect and dis-approval from his classmates and friends, it makes him feel small. This is a teaching moment when a parent or teacher can guide him to modify his actions. It may appear that the choleric isn't recep-tive to your feedback or your opinion, but if you are calm, consis-tent, reasonable, and fair, the child will quietly take it in. You may be surprised when months or years later he lets you know that he heard you.

When the Child Gets Upset

In the choleric's early life, it is the adults who must contain and moderate his more extreme tendencies. In conversation with thera-pist and Waldorf teacher Mimi Devens, she observed that if the parent corrects the choleric publicly, he will stubbornly fight against all attempts at correction. The best way to work with the choleric temperament is to acknowledge his point of view (not necessarily agree with it, but acknowledge it). Let him know that you hear him. He needs to be shown respect so you can deflect the intensity of his anger and get his attention. After the upset, when things are calmed down, parents can go through the steps to show him what he was responsible for in the upsetting incident.

When the choleric child is upset and fuming, it is easy to get sucked into his fire and lose your own cool. This temperament does not respond well to criticism, so stay in control of your own reactions by being reasonable and fair. It is essential to funnel his energy in a way that is productive and measurable. Be sure to affirm his position and then challenge him to do better.

Use Humor to Teach the Choleric

Nothing is achieved by admonition, but much through humor. If the parent or teacher perceives that the choleric child is ready to receive humor, he or she can put on a funny choleric act that will allow the child to see his own funny characteristics and relate them to himself. Of course you don't want to do this in the heat of a dramatic moment, or in a public way that could be perceived as humiliating.

Stand Up to Unacceptable Behavior

Your choleric child can be very intimidating—he slams doors, glares at people, and challenges every opinion that is expressed. He has a tendency to bark orders and charge ahead, never bothering to see whose feelings are getting hurt in the process. It is important that parents and teachers look the choleric child in the eye and "lay down the law." Standing up to the choleric can be exhausting, so parents may want to carefully choose which issues to take on with this child, without sacrificing consistency. The way adults can make the choleric child feel he is supported is by meeting unacceptable behavior head on. He also needs them to spend time reflecting with him.

Thomas Poplawski relates this story in *Renewal* magazine:

> *A choleric ninth grader started the semester by disrupting the class and interrupting the instructor. The teacher took the boy aside immediately after class, looked him straight in the eye, and clearly let him know that if he interrupted the class one more time with his behavior, he would be kicked out of class for the rest of the term. The boy became a model student in that class and couldn't do enough for the teacher.*

If adults or peers have confidence in themselves to face the choleric fearlessly, he will respect them and will abandon his egoism. He needs adults who won't overreact, and ultimately they will become a role model for him.

Find Your Own Inner Choleric

For a choleric adult it is not a great challenge to "fight fire with fire," but even choleric adults must use skill, clarity, and self-control. The adult can understand, effectively meet, and contain the choleric child's fierce energy by facing up to him and letting him know that there is a grown-up in charge. Parents with less forceful temperaments will need to center themselves, mobilize their energy, and have the strong presence required to meet the choleric youngster. It is important to remember that we cannot expect from a child what we ourselves are unable to do, so self-control and loving understanding are essential if we wish to win the choleric child's respect and attention.

Positive Outlets for Choleric Energy in the Classroom

If the teacher notices a restlessness developing in the choleric child, she should find a way to release the tension before the breaking point. Ask the child to clean the blackboard, help move the furniture, or any other *meaningful* chore. This child will work hard when an adult recognizes his potential, so don't try to "busy" a choleric student with meaningless tasks; he'll reject them outright. He loves to be heroic. Find a way for him to achieve a productive, measurable goal, and then allow him to show other students how to achieve the same goal; this is very fulfilling for the choleric temperament.

Mona Lewis, Waldorf handwork teacher, recognized that a disruptive choleric student needed an opportunity to prove himself and challenged him to knit something quite complicated in twenty minutes. Beaming after he received her acknowledgement for succeeding, he became much more attentive and helpful in her class. Let the choleric child know you are counting on him. You can ask him to help move furniture for a dinner party, dig holes for the new garden, or organize other youngsters for a small fundraiser to give him an opportunity to prove himself.

Help Choleric Children Set Priorities, Collaborate, and Delegate

Your child can easily become overcommitted because in his opinion the job won't be done right if he doesn't do it. As the world's self-ordained mover and shaker, it is difficult for this temperament to establish boundaries or say no to a request. This is particularly true of older children and teenagers. Parents can help this child not to become exhausted by assuring him the job can be done by someone else, and by promising that he will be consulted from time to time by the person taking on the task.

One of the most essential skills for the choleric child/teenager to learn is how to collaborate. It is too easy for him to be the pushiest, loudest voice in the room (which is never appreciated by others), so parents are encouraged to help the choleric develop delegation and collaboration skills. It will take time, but with these disciplines in place, the choleric child can become a truly gifted leader.

Overcoming "No!"

Some choleric children have a tendency to say "no" too often, and they require a different approach from the child who says yes to everything. "No" as a first reaction means that he does not like to be surprised (similar to the phlegmatic temperament). "No" is a way to buy time, and a parent working with this aspect of the choleric temperament should take the time to help him envision what is being asked of him. Like the phlegmatic, he will need some moments to mull things over so he can change his mind.

DEVELOPING EGO STRENGTH AND LEADERSHIP

The Importance of Leadership Training: The Stakes Are High

Choleric children have the potential within their temperament to be the leaders of the future, and it is the role of parents and teachers to help them master the undisciplined aspects of the temperament without squelching their leadership potential. It is crucial that adults consciously work to cultivate the positive side of the choleric's temperament, teaching patience, coping skills, and empathy. The choleric can be a creative and enterprising presence in any group, organization, or initiative. The halls of Congress, the boardrooms of large corporations, and professional sports teams are filled with cholerics. However, this temperament left unchecked can lead to behavior that is personally and socially destructive. Youth detention centers and prisons serve as collection points for undisciplined cholerics.

Appeal to Their Hidden Chivalrous Nature

It is always wise to appeal to the chivalrous and heroic nature that this type hides beneath a sometimes forbidding exterior. By assuming that the choleric child possesses these qualities, a parent or teacher can encourage and challenge him to live up to their expectations. Magnanimity and generosity are two virtues of this temperament, and it is merely a matter of bringing them out. This can be done by acknowledging to the choleric child that you know his virtuous side exists. An adult choleric encouraged a better attitude in a younger choleric with the statement, "You know you really have it in you to behave better than that. It doesn't become you not to be your best."

Demand of Yourself What You Would Demand of Others

One goal for parents and teachers working with a choleric child is to first recognize his leadership gifts, and then to encourage him to develop the integrity to demand of himself what he demands of others. Help him understand that if he wants to direct others, he must first learn to discipline himself. Leading by example instead of bullying means he is working out of his evolved choleric nature. By acknowledging that you "know" your child has the courage and ability to take upon himself the demands he makes of others, you are treating him appropriately.

The Importance of Learning Sportsmanship

Unless he is organizing them, the choleric child will find non-competitive games boring. He needs lots of opportunity to release his exuberant energy through games and sports, and vigorous physical activity teaches him how to "wrestle with life." The choleric loves to test himself against others and enjoys overwhelming his opponents; so once again, this will be an opportunity to challenge him to play fair. When his behavior is out of control, remind him privately that he isn't living up to his own high standards. Always help him to maintain dignity, and never reprimand him in public.

Appropriately Appreciating this Child

Choleric children (and adults) are interesting because they want to be unique, and their own individuality is extremely important to them. Ironically, they are utterly dependent on others for appreciation. It seldom occurs to him that in order to gain the right to rule, he must first learn to control himself and to recognize his own faults and shortcomings. He must also learn to recognize and appreciate the talents, gifts, and roles of others. Parents can appeal to this temperament's "ideal" self as a way to help him win self-control and overcome shortcomings. Recognize his gifts or his leadership abilities, and then challenge him to behave at a higher standard.

Allow the Child or Teenager
to Take Responsibility for Misbehavior

If the child is misbehaving, the parent can ask, "What would you do? What do you think your punishment should be?" The child feels this as an appeal to his sense of self; now the decision to do the right thing is his own. A choleric friend shared this story:

> *He came home from a middle-school football event one night long after curfew and quite drunk. His father confronted him when he got home with a neutral but strict demeanor and asked him what he thought his punishment should be. To this day our friend admires the wisdom his father exhibited and is convinced*

that his own suggested punishment was much worse than any-thing his father would have come up with.

Give the Choleric Challenging Tasks

Opposition, competition, and rivalry are food for the choleric's soul. "I wonder if you can do it" is an effective and engaging way to challenge most choleric children. If the child is especially competitive, then a more strongly worded challenge will work. This child needs resistance to overcome and to understand that there are difficulties in life. Bring out the positive aspects of his exuberant energy and confidence by helping him funnel his energy into meaningful tasks that will challenge him.

RESPECTING ADULTS

Earning the Child's Respect

Respect and regard for authority are important to the choleric child, but they will never be given to the position (teacher, parent, boss), only to the person who has earned it. It is essential to this temperament that parents keep their promises, that they say what they mean and mean what they say. A parent that leads by example becomes a significant role model for him, so demonstrating respect for others teaches the choleric how to be respectful.

Choleric Children Need a Hero

It is good for children to believe that their teachers know what they are talking about. The choleric child in particular needs a hero. Respect and esteem for what a person in authority has accomplished are nourishment for the soul. Children want an adult they can trust and respect to be in charge. It is a tall order, but the teacher (or parent) must show that he is well informed, and must not display weakness. The teacher should appear to know everything and be able to do everything and without obviously bragging, point out his own superiority.

In meeting the choleric child, we are likely meeting a future pioneer, leader, or innovator. This thought may not be a solace to an adult dealing with a seven-year-old girl who absolutely refuses to put her coat on, or a young boy who has just pushed his classmate into the wall. But, it is the adults who will help a child of any temperament to find a way to moderate his natural negative tendencies. Within the choleric child's temperament is a hero waiting to be recognized, challenged, and appreciated.

THE CHOLERIC ADULT

DEVELOPING EFFECTIVE RELATIONSHIPS

"It is one thing to show your child the way,
and a harder thing to then stand out of it."
—**Robert Brault**

The Three Stages of the Adult Choleric Temperament

The first-stage choleric is controlling, demanding, and can't stand criticism. He can be quite stubborn and insist on his own way. He wants to be respected, but his Achilles heel is an inability to listen to and accept the views of others. He is socially competitive and he expects to be first. He will take on a great deal of responsibility with energy, enthusiasm, and determination because he believes he is the only one who can do the job right. Whereas the melancholic lives in the past, and the phlegmatic and sanguine live in the present, the choleric lives in the future. The first-stage choleric is extremely goal-oriented and is happy only when accomplishing something.

When other people move too slowly or get in the way of his goal, the choleric can become bossy and pushy. This is particularly uncomfortable for others if the choleric is involved in a team sport or group project. The choleric is confident in his intelligence and strength and isn't afraid to tackle anything. The first-stage choleric is like a military general; he just naturally must take charge.

At the second stage, the *life-experience* stage, the choleric begins to show interest and even respect for other people. He starts to recognize that other people have intelligence, skill, and expertise. At this point in his development, the choleric adult still feels he can do things better than anyone else, and this self-assurance makes him believe he has the right to "rule" others, while refusing to be ruled. However, he does begin to sense that he can't always be in charge. He craves respect and recognition from others, and when he recognizes that his actions make him unpopular, the behavior begins to be modified.

At the third stage, the choleric has learned (perhaps by going through a personal crisis or failure) to respect other people. He has learned that he must demand of himself what he demands of others—but this is difficult for the choleric to do as long as he can blame someone else. The choleric temperament is the stuff kings, presidents, and CEOs are made of, and one's subjects, constituents, and coworkers have a right to demand much of their ruler. If self-control, courage, generosity, and integrity have been developed at this stage, the choleric will have become a "gentle ruler" who uses his skills and organizing abilities to benefit others. He has learned to subordinate himself and rejoices in the accomplishments of others. The choleric parent at this stage will know how to motivate his child from the child's point of view. He is then willing to step back, learn what the child has to teach him, and watch his child flourish.

THE CHOLERIC PARENT

The choleric temperament expresses itself powerfully. To children the choleric adult can seem like an aggressive and strong presence. If you have dominant choleric tendencies, you will most likely have a robust opinion about what is best for your child. Choleric adults tend to be goal-oriented, results-driven extraverts. "If only he or she would do what I say, everything would work out beautifully." It is important to remember that your child possesses strengths that you don't have. Please give him space so his own abilities can flourish. The danger of a choleric parent exerting such a strong and/or domineering ego is the risk of stifling the ego development of the child. Depending on the temperament of the child, this can manifest in several problematic ways.

WHEN THE CHOLERIC PERSONALITY IS TOO IMPOSING

- A *phlegmatic* or *melancholic* child may either close down or become submissive. The phlegmatic child may develop stomachaches under pressure.
- The *melancholic* could develop strong resentments toward the parent or a tendency toward passive-aggressive behavior later on. The melancholic child lives in the past and has a long memory, especially for slights, insults, and hardships.
- The *sanguine* child will either ignore a demand or lie in the face of what they perceive to be strong commands from an adult.
- Any of the temperaments may show signs of nervousness when confronted with too much choleric intensity. It may well manifest as depression in a melancholic, isolation in a phlegmatic, anxiety in a sanguine, and anger and aggression in a choleric, and regression in any child.
- The *choleric* child will likely become rebellious and disobedient in the face of strong demands, even if the demands are well intentioned. This is likely to signal the beginning of a long battle of wills.
- When feeling too imposed upon, any child can become angry and frustrated. In adolescence this power struggle is a sure recipe for disaster. Adolescence is the time for the parent to begin to guide, collaborate, and partner more with their teen,

and to let go gradually so the teen is able to make more decisions with guidance.

When Working with Your Child, You Want to Be an Authority Figure, but Not Authoritarian

The choleric parent loves followers that he can organize and order about. It is important to recognize the difference between authority and power. The parent who operates as a loving authority is prepared for what is to happen at any given time of day because he exerts a conscious influence over his children. This is a different gesture from the parent who is exerting instinctive power. Any child will find a greater sense of security when they know they are being taken care of by someone who is in charge and in control. They can relax, knowing someone will make all the right decisions and choices and tend to their needs. However, a child, no matter what the temperament, will inevitably balk at being controlled for the sake of control. Therapist Mimi Devens advises parents and teachers to avoid the trap of engaging in power struggles, which result from exerting ego. Rather, you as the adult must be the loving, creative ego presence, knowing you are the authority on behalf of the children's best interest.

- The *phlegmatic* child's temperament is not designed to be a member of the troop, so "bossing" the phlegmatic child will not motivate him.
- The *sanguine* child will go along with the program when she can sense the fun and feel loved.
- Any insensitivity on the part of the choleric parent will result in the *melancholic* child becoming deeply wounded and sulky.
- The *choleric* child will respond well to authority because he needs someone bigger than himself to lay down expectations.

Take the time to be a loving authority who behaves respect-fully toward your choleric child.

Your Child Needs You to Slow Down

- The *sanguine* child has difficulty staying focused; therefore the choleric adult will need to devote some time to work with her completion issues.
- The *phlegmatic* child moves very slowly and may take a long time to make a decision. Being hurried disrupts his rhythm and threatens his comfort zone. This is an opportunity for a choleric parent to slow down and develop patience. If you don't, the phlegmatic child may well go into survival mode by digging in and becoming even slower or more immobile. If you absolutely don't have the patience to shop for clothes at your phlegmatic child's extremely slow pace, recruit a close relative who loves shopping.
- The sensitive *melancholic* child gives the choleric parent an opportunity to take a breath and develop patience and objective listening skills. The melancholic needs validation and compassion, while the choleric parent tends toward impatience with complaints. Let this child know you understand how she feels, without agreeing that she is "right "or trying to "fix" what you think ails her. "If that happened to me, I'd feel that way, too." "It's understandable that you feel this way." The melancholic child will feel satisfied if she knows she has been heard. Since melancholic children are by nature sensitive and self-involved, treating them with understanding also teaches them how to be compassionate with others. This is the key to navigating what is painful for the melancholic.

The challenge for the choleric parent: At the end of the day, your children want to know that you can handle what they are telling you without overreacting. They want to know that you are still going to love them even if they had a bad day.

MELANCHOLIC: THE WOUNDED HEALER

Sheltered under the forest's green canopy
Stands a lonely pond.
In her Winter mood, she wishes for the sun
To warm her watery depths.
She dreams of wildlife playing along her banks,
But none appear. And so the pond sits and waits,
Sighing a song of separation that no one hears.

After an eternity of longing,
A sudden wind kisses the pond's surface,
Whispering a message of Spring's return,
And the promise of new beginnings,
Reminding the lonely pond
The forest could not flourish without
The blessing of her life-giving waters.

—**Judith Haney and Bari Borsky**

On the playground, the child who is often found at the edge of the group, watching other children play and feeling left out, will be the melancholic. When she does finally venture forth and something goes amiss (she gets hit by a ball or is ridiculed), the young melancholic child will run away crying to her teacher or parent. From her perspective, someone else is at fault ("he hit me" or "she called me names"). Although this temperament often blames others for her own upsets, she also tends to assume the blame when it is meant for others and will punish herself when she is not at fault. This lack of objectivity keeps her perpetually uncomfortable with others.

The melancholic temperament is related to the earthy, bony element, so this personality is not soft and pliable, but is rather inflexible. The body is on the tall, lanky side, and even though not actually heavy like the phlegmatic, the body *feels* heavy. The child finds it hard to get up in the morning. It is a big effort to wash and get dressed; in fact, it is difficult to move much at all. The body feels *so* heavy, as if there is a resistance that opposes whatever the child wants to do, and it takes much effort and energy to manage it properly. One can see the pain of the struggle in the face of this child—the eyes are sad, the mouth and shoulders droop, and when walking, the child is usually looking at the ground. With her feet dragging, even walking seems to be an effort. A general lack of vitality leads her to actually feel ill much of the time. Each new day is seen as a possibility for failure, and it takes will power to face it. The effort is exhausting and it is as if the youngster were middle-aged instead of very young.

A good example of this temperament is Eeyore, from the Winnie the Pooh stories. We often find him by himself musing on the sad state of his existence, which is not his idea of happy perfection. When Pooh asks, "How are you?" Eeyore responds, "Not very how. I don't seem to have felt at all how for a long time." This poor melancholic fellow wants lots of sympathy, and so does the child with melancholic tendencies.

Raising the melancholic child can be a challenge. She is quiet and withdrawn and is engrossed in the past. She tends to feel that everything is sad and gloomy and places herself at the center of her world, demanding pity. She can be quite thin-skinned, seeing insult where there is none, and has a long memory that doesn't forget slights, hurts, or perceived meanness. The wound may remain for years, and the melancholic in the child may lash out like a sniper when one doesn't expect it.

Fortunate is the melancholic that has for a role model an adult whose life is filled with hard experiences that have been overcome, and who is willing to share his life lessons with the child. By the sympathy that arises for the person of authority, and in the sharing of the justifiably painful destiny, the melancholic can develop into a sympathetic, helpful adult. The youngster in whom sympathies are aroused will happily provide assistance and comfort to the one who needs it. With the helpful support and understanding of parents and teachers, she can learn to be nurturing and compassionate. The gifts of helpfulness and gentleness come from a deep source and once awakened, can lead to sacrifice and committed service to others.

HOW TO RECOGNIZE THE MELANCHOLIC TEMPERAMENT

Physical Expression

The melancholic temperament is expressed through the bony system, which is stiff and heavy. She must be master of her body if she wishes to use it productively, but the melancholic child feels that she cannot manage the body effectively and is not its master.

- Her body feels difficult to move. Her walk is measured and steady, but generally her steps lack firmness and seem to drag her along.
- Her facial features can often appear to be weary and concerned, and suffering often shows in her eyes.
- This child is physically hypersensitive and will typically share with her parents or teacher every ache and pain. She is touchy about the way things feel and will whine about tight-fitting

clothes, scratchy fabrics, and temperature extremes. She has a preference for comfortable clothing, often choosing somber colors to match her mood.

- She is sensitive to cold water, and she loves warmth, both inner and outer. The melancholic appreciates being looked after by an adult as a source of inner warmth, and she requires adequate clothing for outer warmth.
- She is fussy about food and will take a while to adopt new tastes. She may manipulate others to obtain her preferred sweets.

INWARD EXPRESSION

A child with a dominant melancholic temperament is introverted. She is easily affected by her environment and how she believes the world treats her. Because of her heightened sensitivity, the melancholic child's version of an incident, which she believes to be true, may not agree with how others perceived it.

- Where other children might find excitement, or challenge, this child sees obstacles, which then fulfill her prophecy that life is hard and people want to make it difficult for her. One emotionally wrought seventh-grade student came running to her teacher during recess complaining loudly, "Mrs. P.! Mrs. P.! Johnny *almost* insulted me!"
- She believes her experiences are peculiar to her and that such things can and do happen *only* to her.
- The melancholic child is serious, quiet, and withdrawn. She may spend a great deal of time reflecting on her experiences and can be engrossed in the past. There is a tendency to replay past negative occurrences in her mind.
- She often sees each day as a possibility for failure, and it takes will power for her to face it. This process can be exhausting.

- Children with a dominant melancholic temperament take refuge in sleep. They are always tired and feel they don't get enough rest. As they do not look forward to greeting the day, it takes a long time to get out of bed. It can be fatiguing for them to think about what challenges the day ahead might bring.

- A general lack of vitality gives support to her feeling unwell. If you ask how she is, you will get a list of issues. This quality of endless complaining is a characteristic of the immature melancholic adult as well. Sharing her internal misery gives her pleasure. Receiving sympathy for her plight can contribute to her belief that others care about her.

SOCIAL EXPRESSION

The melancholic child is the one hanging on the edge of a group, not sure how to join in. She is often shy and finds casual social interactions troublesome. She is slow to make friends and generally gravitates toward others of a similar temperament.

- When the melancholic child finally does trust someone, she is deeply loyal to that person.

- The melancholic has a long memory for slights. She can be easily hurt by what others say about her, or what she believes they say about her, and will in turn retaliate by hurting others. If the offender apologizes, she won't be as likely to retaliate.

- The melancholic can tear up her work because it does not meet her high standards, or she can stop halfway because it is not going to be "good enough" anyway. This perfectionism makes it hard for her to laugh at herself or to feel she is the cause of anything negative. When something goes wrong, it is always someone else's fault. It is difficult for the melancholic child to admit wrongdoing and apologize because then she would feel small and would not consider herself perfect.

- On the other hand, the melancholic child tends to assume blame when it is meant for someone else. She may be filled with guilt and punish herself even when she is not at fault. This lack of clarity about herself gives her an unbalanced relationship to the world.

FAMILY DYNAMICS

The melancholic personality tends to worry about everything. This child is self-involved and often does not hear what the other person is saying. She hangs on to details but misses the main point. This can be frustrating for parents because she may argue that the parent didn't say x, y, z due to the fact that she only heard the beginning or the end, but not the middle of the conversation.

- The melancholic is often teased and annoyed by her siblings because she lacks a sense of humor. She can take things too personally and will await an opportunity to strike back, often by tattling. This child experiences satisfaction when "they" get into trouble.

- Melancholics respond compassionately to a hurt or sick animal and will lovingly care for it. If the animal dies, she will blame herself, often for years afterward.

- She enjoys helping her parents with small jobs, such as figuring the mileage covered on a trip, how much money was spent, or what items are needed at the grocery store.

- These children are often voracious readers and should be encouraged to read the biographies of successful personalities who have overcome difficult trials. This helps them develop compassion for others. It will also demonstrate that they are not the only ones to have negative experiences in life.

- Hobbies can include reading, painting, jigsaw puzzles, and solo card games. In arithmetic, the melancholic has the closest relationship to subtraction. This seems to agree with her tendency to focus on what she does not have, rather than what she does; or what is leaving her life, rather than what is entering.

- The musical instrument of greatest appeal may be the stringed instruments, because deep feelings can be expressed through playing them.

HOW TO WORK WITH THE MELANCHOLIC CHILD

Because the melancholic child cannot overcome her own self-involvement without the help of others, she can sometimes feel like a burden to her friends and family. However, once this trait has been overcome, there is no hesitation on the part of the mature melancholic to make sacrifices for the good of others. The melancholic child teaches us to understand and have empathy for our fellow human beings.

MANAGE THE SUFFERING

Deconstruct the Negative Experiences

The melancholic temperament has a tendency to represent her experiences from a negative perspective. She is often overwhelmed with dark feelings and is unable to separate her emotions from the facts of a situation. Mimi Devens, therapist and Waldorf teacher, advises that a cognitive-therapy approach can help with this. When your child complains that "it was a terrible day," help her to break the day down into small bites. "Was it terrible on the playground today?" "You had math today. Was that terrible?" "You played baseball today. Was that terrible?" Continue until you can identify the one incident that "rained on her parade" and caused the whole day to seem terrible. Then you can honestly declare, "Wow, it sounds like most of the day was OK, but in singing class you felt terrible...is that about right?" "Deconstructing" the day helps put things in perspective for the child. Going through this process repeatedly is good training for your child. She can use this skill for the rest of her life.

Teach Your Child to Solve Problems

Once the "terrible" incident of the day has been identified, be sure to illustrate how the situation might be improved next time. If Johnny yelled at her for taking his pencil off the desk, encourage her to ask him for permission first next time. Spending the time to practice solving these problems with your melancholic child will help her to feel safe. It is helpful to remember that there is always a solution, and the child is part of it. You can also remind her of successful experiences she's had with similar situations. "I remember last month Suzy was upset with you because she dropped her notebook when you bumped into her. And then you apologized, picked up the notebook, and gave it back to her, and even gave her a few pieces of clean paper from your notebook. Remember how grateful she was, and how good it made you feel?"

Work with What Is: Allow the Suffering

No one wants to see their child suffer, but it is important to remember that this temperament sees the sad and difficult side of life: she cannot be talked out of her inner distress. This temperament experiences suffering on a more profound level than the other temperaments. Within limits, one should allow the melancholic her misery, always affirming and supporting, without trying to "change" her.

Bari's story:

While presenting an overview of the four temperaments to a group of coaches, I mentioned that the melancholic temperament comes into the world to experience suffering in herself and in others, and it is a mistake to try to "jolly" the melancholic child out of her gloomy world outlook. When we work appropriately with the melancholic child, she will learn compassion for the afflictions of others. The next day, one of the coaches, who has a melancholic temperament (I will call her Diane), sent me a note thanking me for giving her permission to be who she really is. When I questioned her about what this meant to her, Diane said that she could now accept that she wasn't like other people... bubbly and happy, like the sanguine, or driven and extraverted like the choleric. She said that she could now work comfortably and successfully within the parameters of her own melancholic temperament. The power of understanding her temperament was transformative. Within a short time Diane changed her hairstyle, wore more colorful clothing, and landed a job where she was appreciated and respected. She became more accepting of herself and of others; she clearly moved from feeling less than effective, to feeling empowered to use the strength of her temperament to be of service to others.

Do Not Console the Melancholic

The melancholic is difficult to console, but she responds well to understanding and, like everyone else, she wants to have her feelings validated. Both child and adult see the sad and gloomy side of life, and attempts to make light of her dark point of view will be rebuffed and considered frivolous. Waldorf teacher Bonnie Holden advises parents not to try to jolly their melancholic child out of her sour mood or try to make her "feel better." Comments such as "I can understand how you would feel that way," or "I would feel bad if that happened to me, too," would be appropriate. However, avoid getting distressed or overwhelmed yourself. This would not help the child learn how to deal with her sorrow in a healthy way. She needs to experience an objective response to her misery, which she can use as an example for her future behavior. The best course of action is to point out other people's suffering so that attention is drawn outward and away from the child's own self-absorption.

Help to Externalize the Dark Images in the Imagination

What the melancholic child needs is an appropriate way to bring into the light what lives in the dark of her soul. This child is an introvert, and it is healthy to help her externalize "menacing things." If the child has seen a scary movie or heard a frightening story, it is good to ask for details about what was seen or heard. It is important that she bring the images out into the open so they don't expand their importance in her inner life. She can be encouraged to write a story or draw a picture of the event, and/or create a poem about her inner experience.

The melancholic lives strongly in her day-to-day trauma. One way to help her move through her fear, self-pity, or self-involvement is to encourage her to feel sorry for someone else. Mona Lewis, Waldorf School handwork teacher, advises that when the child is young, feeling compassion for another can be accomplished through made-up bedtime stories and "fairy tales." Create a bedtime story with a protagonist that has the same trauma as the melancholic child, and make sure the trauma gets resolved by the end of the story. Giving voice to fears a child cannot put expression to will help resolve the fear and allow the child to settle down and fall asleep.

> In working with her own melancholic daughter Mona created a fairy named "Dew Drop," and Dew Drop was afraid that other children would laugh at her, or that her wings had gotten dirty, or that she would never escape from the tree. By naming the fear and making it sound commonplace, the melancholic child experiences some resolution.

Melancholic children travel to dark depths, and they don't easily talk about their fears. Parents can do a couple of things to help mitigate (but not release) their gloom. Permeate the home atmosphere with an "all is well" attitude. Stay positive, acknowledge the child's fear indirectly (they don't want anyone to know their weakness), and keep seeing their beauty.

Help Her Experience that She Is Not Alone

The melancholic child feels that her experiences are not shared by anyone else. More advice from Mona: "When my daughter would go into her bedroom and stuff down whatever was bothering her, I took my knitting into the bedroom, and without saying a word, I sat in the room with my daughter just knitting. After about twenty or thirty minutes of silence, my melancholic daughter began to open up and talk." A parent's message should be: "I'm here for you no matter what," and "I see you, I love you unconditionally, and I want what is best for you." This allows the melancholic child to let down her guard so the thoughts and words can be released.

If you can lighten her burden by letting her know she isn't the only one in the world who feels this way, you give the melancholic a safe space to figure things out for herself. You cannot tell a melancholic what to do, but you can support her by not being shocked by her pain and by loving her for who she is.

Share about Overcoming Your Own Painful Experiences

It is good for the parent to share with the child the pain and suffering which the parent has overcome. Judy's story:

Once I overheard my boyfriend saying really hurtful things about me. I thought life would never be the same. I was inconsolable. After several days I got up enough courage to ask him why he said those awful things. He told me that he wasn't talking about me; he was talking about another person who was giving him trouble. And he admonished me, ever so nicely, not to eavesdrop!

Sharing such stories enables the child to sympathize and demonstrates that most problems are not insurmountable. This should only be attempted if the parent's difficulties were genuine, because the melancholic child is attuned to insincerity. Don't burden a child with stories of difficulties that the parent has not yet truly overcome.

Help the melancholic to realize that other people have similar problems. She believes that she is unique, which can cause her to cultivate a sense of separateness. Age-appropriate biographical stories encourage such a child to break out of her self- preoccupation and allow her to take an interest in the lives and concerns of others. It can be therapeutic to read how others overcame their hardships and unhappiness to lead full, helpful lives. Helen Keller's story is one good example; also President Roosevelt's struggle with polio.

Effective Parenting and Environment

Routine Is Important

A consistent routine can go a long way toward providing a sense of security for the melancholic child. Be sensitive to the fact that resistance to change could be disguised fear. By giving your child plenty of warning for any anticipated changes and explaining that her whole world is not changing, with just these few details (a change of plans or activities, or a new responsibility for the child), you will help her to feel secure. Parents should give special attention to any alteration in the environment, such as a change in room color or living conditions. Help your child to know that she is safe. Encourage her to develop healthy routines from early on: daily piano practice, homework completed before going out to play, keeping her clothes clean and organized, and so forth.

Handling Serious Family Problems

Serious family problems have an especially strong effect on the melancholic child. Her response may be denial that anything is happening. She takes guilt on herself for a family death or divorce. During a divorce she feels the world is collapsing around her. A parent needs to tell the child as much as she can tolerate. This will depend partly on her age. She should be told enough about the situation so her guilt is softened and some sense of security is restored. Give some details, expected time lines, how life may be different later, and how it may remain the same, giving special emphasis to the fact that she has done nothing wrong and that Mom and Dad will continue to love her and take very good care of her.

Learn to Set Limits

Parents should be supportive but firm. They have to be careful not to indulge and, at the same time, not to ignore the child. In his article "The Melancholic Child, Gifts and Challenges," Thomas Poplawski states that research has shown that the over-protective style of parenting exacerbates the melancholic child's uncertainty, while the "limit-setting" approach reduces inhibition and fearfulness.

Encourage Facing Unpleasant Situations

The melancholic child often wants to stay home from school to avoid any number of problems, real or imagined. It's just too much trouble to make the effort required. Parents should be mindful not to encourage escape from unpleasant situations. Absences separate the child from the rest of the class and increase the feeling of alienation, making it that much harder to re-establish relationships. Review the situation with the child, drawing as many details from her as possible. Then make suggestions as to how to deal with each detail. The child wants parental support in taking apart her perceived problem, and it will seem easier to handle one detail at a time. Judy tells her story:

> *Starting at eight years old, I played softball in our small Ohio town. I was the outfielder who prayed that no one could bat the ball out that far, because I was convinced I would be badly hurt if I tried to catch it. This avoidance seemed to serve me until I entered high school, where I had to play softball for an entire four-month semester. Realizing I had to do something about this fear, I asked my Dad to throw balls at me until I wasn't afraid anymore. He started close, throwing softly, and gradually went farther away and threw harder. We practiced for several days, until I was confident that I could safely catch a high fly. To this day, I am so grateful to him for spending that time with me to improve myself and banish that fear.*

Encourage Socialization

Gently encourage your melancholic to visit friends and/or have friends over to your house. Early training in socializing with others may help to weaken the tendency to prefer being alone in later life. Let her help you prepare for your next dinner party so she can see what tasks need to be completed for a successful evening.

Maintain an Orderly Environment

A typical melancholic child wants order, both in her life and with her belongings. She can be spiteful if a younger sibling destroys her things. Work alongside your child to keep her room in order. This will help with bonding and make her feel special.

Movement and Warmth

Warmth, both inner and outer, is a necessity for this child. All children should be encouraged to eat healthy meals and to exercise each day, and this is especially true for the melancholic, who would prefer to live on sweets. Movement helps to break the spell of gloominess, so encourage a bike ride, a walk in the neighborhood, or a swim to get her out of a dreary mood.

Sweets Make Her More Comfortable

This personality's taste for sweets may be indulged because sweets help the child feel inwardly comfortable and less irritable. Sweeteners such as honey, dark maple syrup, or molasses, rather than refined sugar, are suitable for this purpose in small doses.

Help This Child to Feel Needed

When she is old enough, include the melancholic in preparing for a dinner party by asking her to do the dishes or set the table. Your melancholic child would prefer to be helpful behind the scenes rather than to do the entertaining. It is important to let her know she is needed and how important her contribution is, but it must be genuine. Make the tasks meaningful or she will refuse to do them.

Ask Her Opinion

The melancholic responds warmly if asked for her opinion on something. Draw her attention to the outer world and awaken her interest in it, through discussions of outward events and people.

Help Her to Overcome Feeling Bullied

Bullying is a serious problem in many schools, and it is not uncommon for melancholic children to be bullied. Should this happen to your child, help her to understand that her reactions (over-sensitivity) might encourage or prolong the bullying. Help her learn not to react, or find a way of expressing herself other than whining. At the same time, assure her that you understand how she feels. Relating personal stories of how you, or someone close to you, overcame being teased or bullied will help her understand that she is not the only one this happens to. Melancholic children learn by example, so give her examples of how other people have handled similar situations. Stay awake to the fact that your melancholic may actually be having a terrible time at the hands of a bully and that you may need to intervene.

Teach Her How She Causes Suffering in Others

The consequences of her actions must be brought home to her, particularly as they affect others and cause them suffering. Show her how her morose attitude affects others. Point out her unsympathetic responses, and ask how she would like it if someone else acted that way toward her.

Give the Child Obstacles and Challenges

When a challenge arises, the melancholic temperament tends to see it as insurmountable and can easily give up. It is an effective practice to give the child opportunities to practice overcoming obstacles. Start small and work up to more difficult tasks over time so she gets a sense of accomplishment to bolster the next, larger effort. For instance, when you ask her to put her toys away, remain in the room and offer encouragement to finish the (seemingly) insurmountable task. "That certainly looked like a huge task, didn't it? But you did it all! Yeah!" Add more difficult challenges as the child ages. Putting difficulties in the child's way helps to guide her away from her normal brooding. Always remind her of past successes.

Do Not Encourage Bargaining

Be prepared to give a straight yes-or-no answer to a request, as the child will find a hundred reasons for some particular action or non-action. Don't encourage bargaining. It is always appropriate, however, to recognize and validate her disappointment.

Teach Perseverance by Setting Goals

Waldorf teacher Bonnie Holden advises parents to encourage the melancholic to persevere by setting clear goals: "Do this for ten minutes." "Do this forty times." If the child knows the exact expectations, there is less chance of her becoming anxious. It is good to start with a small task and then extend it so that your child feels success early on and is not discouraged.

Whatever skills the melancholic is trained to acquire during childhood will make life easier for the future adult. These might include washing the dishes, ironing, vacuuming, cleaning the bathroom, organizing the contents of her drawers, and so forth. Proficiency in these areas adds to a feeling of self-sufficiency, which will be needed later in life. It is a significant accomplishment for the adult melancholic to complete some task as a matter of course or habit, without the feeling that there is a mountain of effort required. The melancholic pays attention to details because she wants her work to be "perfect." She can become discouraged and give up if her work isn't just so. Parents who encourage the child to persevere will help her develop habits for success.

How the Melancholic Learns

The phlegmatic child learns by imitating adult behavior. The choleric child needs to feel respect for an authority figure. The sanguine child will learn from an adult with whom it can develop personal love. The melancholic child learns to develop sympathy when a teacher or other significant adult shares the story of overcoming their own painful destiny. It is by emulating the compassionate response of an evolved melancholic adult, such as a teacher, that this child will blossom in her sympathy and compassion for others.

Make the melancholic in your life aware of other people's struggles. It pulls her out of herself and allows her to look out at the world with compassion. Unlike the choleric, who relates to stories of over-coming great obstacles, the melancholic relates most strongly to other people's suffering. When the melancholic child's sympathies are aroused, she can be very kind and gentle. She is very thoughtful around an ill or injured person, but the person's situation will need to be pointed out to her.

The Importance of Gratitude

In his book *Authentic Happiness*, Dr. Martin Seligman stresses that one positive way to increase happiness is to consciously express gratitude. This is difficult for the melancholic child to do. In extreme cases this inability can manifest as feeling overwhelmed or depressed. Encourage your child to look outward and to con-sciously express gratitude. Focusing on what one has to be grateful for is good training for this personality type, and is a good coping strategy for the adult melancholic as well.

Make Your Child Feel that Her Good Deeds Are Important

In her book *Between Form and Freedom, A Practical Guide for the Teenage Years,* Betty Staley advises that persuading a child to do something for someone else may mean building up the importance of the act—making it very special. The child receives the benefit even if the adult feels too much is being made of it. She will be happy to do something for someone else if the request is put in such a way that she feels she is sacrificing herself. This also helps her to overcome her egoism.

THE MELANCHOLIC ADULT

DEVELOPING EFFECTIVE RELATIONSHIPS

"Do not let what you cannot do interfere with what you can do."
—**John Wooden**, Basketball Coach

THE THREE STAGES OF THE ADULT MELANCHOLIC TEMPERAMENT

The first-stage melancholic could be described as sad, complaining, and needy. The thinking is often negative because her focus is on the sad side of life and she doesn't see the positive aspects of a situation. She wants sympathy and compassion from others, but has little to give herself. Her vitality is low, so she often feels ill. It requires an effort to move her inflexible body through the day. She is sensitive to perceived insults, which she will remember well into the future. Tasks are generally completed with attention to detail, as close to perfection as she is able to achieve. She has few friends, and those she has tend to be similar in personality.

As her egoism lessens, the second-stage melancholic begins to feel compassion for others. This allows her to be more receptive to those who need advice, and she can now exhibit patience while doing so. At this stage the melancholic is emerging from her shell, and if she finds mutual interests with another, she can be an excellent conversationalist. She is less self-occupied when she is deeply involved in her work or with a hobby. Her egoism can be overcome for brief periods, but is not yet sustained. She will continue to experience "crises" as she strives for control over her self-involvement tendencies.

At the third-stage, the melancholic has transformed her pessimism and has become a gentle, caring, loving human being. She no longer complains about others and the world around her, but now appreciates both. She is now grateful for what she has and is less concerned about what she does not. She has finally learned how to develop an interest in others and has found ways to be of service. Caring professions (doctors, teachers, counselors, firefighters, police officers, and so on) are filled with mature melancholics who know that real satisfaction in life comes from helping others.

THE MELANCHOLIC PARENT

The melancholic is always conscious of the pain and suffering in herself and in the world. She is a loner and seeks sympathy from anyone who will listen, but doesn't reciprocate by offering much sympathy for others. If you have a dominant melancholic temperament, there will be a tendency to complain to your children about your troubles and challenges. Contrarily, instead of letting your child learn valuable life lessons by helping them work through their own issues, you may be inclined to smother or over-pamper them. The danger here is that too much focus on the negative will cloud the instinctive sunshine of a child's life. Depending on the temperament of the child, this over-focus, over-fussing tendency can manifest in several problematic ways.

- Living in painful experiences is "normal" from the melancholic's perspective. However, the melancholic parent who encourages her *phlegmatic* child to relive a painful experience will hamper the phlegmatic child's recovery. All children need sympathy when they are hurt or ill, but constant fussing will encourage a concentration on the negative for this already inwardly focused child. The stress this may create could cause digestive problems in the child or a tendency toward hypochondria. It is essential that the melancholic parent recognize her own fears and not project them onto her child. To be effective, the melancholic parent should focus on the outward daily routine of her child to keep him healthy: regular mealtime and bedtime, healthful food, daily exercise. The phlegmatic child tends toward corpulence, so it is unwise to comfort or reward this child with the sweets that the melancholic loves. Foods like cookies, cakes, and pies are too difficult for the phlegmatic child to metabolize.

- The melancholic parent who needs or demands sympathy from her *choleric* children will lose their respect. The choleric child wants an authority with a strong ego presence to bounce against, and has no respect for weak adults. He will run roughshod over the melancholic adult that feels sorry for herself. All children (and especially the choleric child) need to feel that competent parents are in charge of their welfare. Parents should be clear and direct about their expectations of the choleric child because subtle hints about what is or is not wanted will not work.

- The *melancholic* child will feel comforted by the sympathy she receives from a melancholic parent. However, too much pampering could cause this inwardly focused child to become a hypochondriac, or reinforce the belief that the world is filled with pain and misery. A short objective review of the child's trouble, with a comment such as, "I can see how you would feel that way," followed with a hug are all that is required. The parent then needs to divert her child's attention to others who really are in need of help and support, and work with her child to find ways of alleviating the suffering of others—humans or animals. If the parent will join in the activity, it will guide the youngster to look outward instead of inward.

- The melancholic parent will need to learn to "lighten up" when working with her *sanguine* child. The melancholic parent's tendency to constantly worry will cause the sanguine child to withhold information ("I don't want to worry my mother or father") or lie. This naturally sunshiny, outgoing child will feel claustrophobic around a morose parent and will want to escape to a more socially supportive environment (such as a friend's home). She needs her parent to show interest in her current activities, and not be critical if the interests are temporary or the results are not perfect.

The challenge for the melancholic parent: Learn how to see the world through your children's eyes so you can give them the great gift of your compassion and understanding, and then learn when to "let go."

PHLEGMATIC: THE HONEY BEAR

Ocean waves move rhythmically round the earth,
Balancing the cold of the poles with the heat of the equator,
The tides lapping gently against the shores of the world.

When winds collide above, the frenzied water harms all in its path.
When the earth below moves suddenly, tsunamis are created,
Rush toward the land, and cause destruction there.

The storms are soon spent and the tempo of the waves resumed.
The tide continues its rhythmical brush against the shore,
Restoring balance, and slowly reshaping the land.

—Judith Haney

Have you ever observed children at play? At first you notice those who are energetically engaged in running, tumbling, and yelling. Then, if you look a bit more carefully, there will be others who are unaware of the mayhem going on around them because they are engrossed in quietly eating or reading rather than actively playing. The quiet children most likely have a phlegmatic temperament. This child has a body that is heavily built, perhaps even a little flabby, and he looks rather "dreamy." He may seem "unintelligent," but don't be deceived...he just needs extra time to consider everything. The phlegmatic child is perfectly content being "inactive."

Whereas choleric children pound the earth with vigor and intention as they walk, phlegmatic children move slowly. One could say they shamble along and don't seem to be terribly conscious of the ground they walk on, which makes them seem clumsy. There is no point in trying to hurry a phlegmatic child because he has a strong resistance to haste; it's not in his nature to move quickly. Everything takes time with this youngster—walking, eating, learning, decision-making—absolutely everything.

Like Winnie the Pooh, phlegmatics thrive on routine and habit: regular mealtime, regular bath time, and consistent bedtime. He is so deeply embedded in his habits that he needs a few days' warning if his routine will be changed. He tends to overreact to sudden alterations to his schedule, so news about going out to dinner on Friday instead of eating at home should not be sprung at the last minute on the phlegmatic child.

This child tends to demand very little, which makes this temperament seem like the easiest to raise. As long as no one expects him to exert himself, physically or mentally, and his home routine includes regular meal, bed, and bath times, he will be happy. The phlegmatic temperament is strongly related to the earth's water element and his own biological rhythmical elements. When his environmental rhythms are consistent and orderly, and he feels safe and comfortable, this child will be placid as a still lake. However, if he is taken by surprise or pushed beyond his comfort zone, this quiet, easy-going child can react like a hurricane.

Neither the phlegmatic child nor the adult is a "big" personality. He resists the limelight and prefers to work behind the scenes in a support position. As a mature adult he is a faithful and reliable friend, sensitive to the needs of others, and is a comfort to be around. We call him "Honey Bear" because he exudes peace, quiet, stability, and security.

HOW TO RECOGNIZE
THE PHLEGMATIC TEMPERAMENT

Rhythm and Consistency Are Important

Phlegmatic children tend to be introverts. If we think of the tortoise in the fairy tale *The Tortoise and the Hare,* we begin to build the picture of a child that is slow moving, methodical, not particularly energetic, and living comfortably in his own shell.

- Rhythm and consistency are important for all children, but particularly for the phlegmatic child. Without routine this child can become anxious. He understands intuitively that his routine is the way things are supposed to be.

- The phlegmatic child dislikes surprises or a change in routine. Educators have observed that if they give their class a surprise exam, the phlegmatic children will often do poorly. However, if they give the same class advance notice about a test in three days, the same children will do very well. The dictionary defines phlegmatic as having or showing a slow and stolid temperament. This absolutely describes a child with this temperament—until his routine is interrupted or he is taken by surprise. Then he can become very angry or even get "out of control."

- These children really enjoy the customs and rituals of life. Mealtime, story time, and bedtime are enjoyable, comforting experiences as long as the routine is consistent. An adult phlegmatic friend of ours has made a ritual of afternoon tea and cakes no matter what activity or deadline is going on around her.

THE PHLEGMATIC CANNOT BE RUSHED

Inertia can be a challenge for a phlegmatic child, and parents and teachers will find it difficult to get him moving on a task. On the other hand, it can be tricky to get him to stop once he starts a project. This child does not like to leave a job before it is completed to the last detail.

- This temperament dislikes haste in any form: he doesn't want to be pushed to make a decision, solve a math problem, or do a chore. When asking a phlegmatic child or adult a question, he requires time to reflect and think about his answer.

- When he becomes interested in a topic, the normally quiet phlegmatic can become quite animated and chatty. A phlegmatic architect friend of ours admits that he can spend the entire day discussing architecture with colleagues, but as soon as the discussion moves away from architecture, he has nothing to add to the conversation.

- A child who has a dominant phlegmatic personality feels best when living "within himself" and appears to be asleep to the outer world. It is as if there were a veil between the child and the rest of the world. He lives in a kind of fog that prevents him from receiving any really sharp or vivid impressions.

- He enjoys quiet activities like coloring, reading, or playing solitary games.

- With his quiet unhurried way, methodical mind, and self-reflective capacity, the phlegmatic has the greatest possibility of learning self-discipline and acquiring wisdom.

PHYSICAL APPEARANCE

If the child is predominantly phlegmatic, the body is rounded and somewhat flabby. One has the impression that standing very straight takes too much effort. His body lacks energy and he sometimes seems to be half-asleep. His face appears to be quite passive, and the eyes lack sparkle.

- When this personality looks out at the world, he seems not to have much interest in what is going on around him. In fact, he feels best when living within himself. He is focused on his inner comfort, and he enjoys life taken at a sluggish pace, rather than running from one activity to another.

- The sanguine temperament lives strongly in her nervous system, which causes her to be dynamic and lively. It is different for the phlegmatic child because he is influenced by the glandular system, which causes his behavior to be slow. Sleeping, eating, and daydreaming are favorite pastimes.

- Their metabolic nature can cause phlegmatic children to become overweight. Parents will want to pay special attention not to include too many starches and sugars in the diet.

- One hallmark of this temperament is the way they walk. Phlegmatic children "amble" in an unhurried, loose-limbed manner. They seem clumsy because their consciousness doesn't extend all the way to their feet.

RELATIONSHIP TO OTHERS

Socially, the phlegmatic is a little slow to make friends. He can be quite self-indulgent when it comes to inner comfort, and so can't really be bothered to use his energy to relate to other people.

- He lives within himself, but not like the melancholic child, who tends to exclude or ignore others. One could say that it is his nature to be untroubled by what goes on around him. During a discussion or class lesson, the phlegmatic can be completely unaware that others are waiting for him to respond, and he is probably surprised to learn that people think he is ignoring them.

- Being naturally reserved, the phlegmatic child doesn't normally assert himself in social situations; however, if someone will break the ice for him by sweeping him along into an activity with other children, he will mix well. He has an easy-going manner and a good sense of humor. He is happy to listen to other people talk, but doesn't usually have much to add to the conversation.

- He vicariously shares in the interests and enjoyments of his friends, but does not, on his own, express creativity, original-ity, or spontaneity. It's easy to see why children with this tem-perament are not the most exciting of friends. They are gener-ally well-behaved and amenable to whatever goes on as long as they are not made to feel uncomfortable.

- Teachers can help engage phlegmatic children in the activi-ties of the other students. This youngster instinctively prefers to remain passive and static, so parents should organize play dates for their phlegmatic child to help stimulate his absorp-tion of other children's interests.

- The natural stability of this temperament helps to bring bal-ance to the family environment. Although he might seem a little "boring," he is loyal, steady, honest, and truthful. He can be counted on to keep his word.

- Because he is content to live within himself, it may take some effort to get to know him. It also takes more time for the phlegmatic to mature.

Does Not Take on Leadership Roles

Even when asked, this temperament is not comfortable expressing his opinion. He doesn't enjoy jumping into the fray of a noisy family discussion, nor does he want to risk being rebuked, contradicted, or having his view criticized. That is definitely not within his comfort zone. There is always the danger that by giving voice to his thoughts, he will be asked to do something beyond his comfort level.

- There is no desire to stand out from the crowd. He will not grab the limelight, but waits in the wings to congratulate others as they leave the stage.

- The phlegmatic is more at home following rather than leading. If a friend tries something new first, and approves of it, then this child will easily join in. New foods are suspect until the rest of the family agrees they are delicious.

- He doesn't want anyone making demands of him, and he would prefer to stay still and not be bothered. The phlegmatic is suspicious of, and even sad for, those busy bees that are always creating work for themselves.

- Phlegmatics form a solid base of cooperative, rule-abiding, pleasant children. They follow parents' or teachers' orders and they enjoy doing things well.

Takes Things Literally

- This youngster takes everything literally. If asked to dry the dishes, they will be dried carefully and thoroughly, but he will not automatically think to put them away, too.

- He lacks a subtle sense of a situation. If you ask him to do something, he will do exactly what you have asked and nothing more.

Knud Asbjorn Lund tells the story about the phlegmatic housekeeper who was asked to close all the windows in the house in case of rain. The owner of the home suddenly wakes up from an afternoon nap, alarmed because water is leaking through the ceiling. When the owner runs upstairs he discovers that the French doors are wide open. When he confronts the housekeeper, she responds, "But sir, I did what you told me to do. I closed all the windows."

- He will seldom take the initiative to think of what the next step might be when working on a task, but once all the steps are explained to him, he will complete each one with care.

HOW TO WORK WITH THE PHLEGMATIC CHILD

We can associate the word "time" with the phlegmatic temperament. It takes some effort to get to know this child, and he will be a person who matures slowly. There is a tendency for the Hares of the world to rush right past this slow-moving Tortoise, but that would be a mistake because the phlegmatic child and adult have much to teach us. The mature phlegmatic personality is sensitive to others' needs and is a faithful, reliable friend who is comfortable to be around. He knows how to relax and exudes peace and quiet, order, and rhythm.

COMPLETING TASKS AND ACCEPTING CHANGES

Give Your Child Time to Reflect

A signature characteristic of the phlegmatic temperament is that he is slower to respond than the other three temperaments. This child needs time to reflect, ruminate, "gather wool," and think things through. Decisions reached this way will be sensible ones. It takes a while for new ideas to percolate through the mind of the phlegmatic, as it may involve reshaping some already existing ones and rearranging the ideas already in his head to accommodate the new.

Judy tried to institute the "Sunday dinner in the middle of the day" concept when her phlegmatic child was about six years of age, but he would have none of it. Dinner (the big meal of the day) was in the evening every other day of the week, and the idea of dinner time being different on Sunday threw him for a loop. Instituting this timetable when he was only two or three might have allowed him to more easily accept this routine.

A doctor recommended to a phlegmatic friend that she "Breakfast like a king, lunch like a prince, and supper like a pauper." It took her ten years actually to institute this unfamiliar regimen.

Keeping the Child Awake and Focused

These children have difficulty completing their assignments on time because they work slowly, and they tend to be dreamy, so focusing is a challenge. Reminders to get back to the topic at hand may strike one as similar to those needed to keep the sanguine on track. The difference is the sanguine's attention is usually derailed by something else of interest, whereas the phlegmatic child merely loses interest. Parents need to be inventive to get this temperament's attention: call his name, jiggle your keys, slam your hand on the table, etc. Once your child is awake and you have his attention, tell him what he needs to know in a concise manner before he drifts off again.

Do Not Interrupt

The phlegmatic does not react well to interruptions, so once the job has begun, he must be left in peace to finish it on his own. If you must break the concentration of a phlegmatic, understand that there will be an overreaction that is sure to follow. Always give your child due notice of changing requirements. One would be wise to wander along as if by chance and see how the work is going. Admire the good points, and very casually make small alterations as necessary. Let him know when you are satisfied with his work as a way of encouragement.

Prepare Him for Future Events

Your phlegmatic child needs a lot of preview. Information about future events must have time to be digested. Give him ample warning, such as: "In three days we will be having a test," or "In two days we are going out to dinner." Educators have observed that when they drop a surprise test on students, this is the group that will always do poorly. But if the same students are given advance warning, they will do well.

DISCIPLINING THE PHLEGMATIC

Don't Get Upset or Overreact

Because the phlegmatic child inclines toward self-reflection, parents can help alleviate an upset by just talking calmly to him. Gently inquire about what has him upset or what is happening. As with a choleric outburst, reconstruction of the event will be easier after the initial agitation or temper tantrum, so wait until the child calms down.

If Punishment Is Necessary, Be Swift and Concise

If punishment is necessary, it should be immediate, so the deed and the consequences can be connected in his mind. Comments should be concise and to the point, kindly delivered, not emotional or harsh. Be careful not to use guilt with this child. According to Betty Staley in her book *Soul Weaving*, guilt is valid only when the child can say "I can't believe I did that" and can assess his action, not his "self."

Obeying Orders

Unlike the other three temperaments, a phlegmatic child can be given orders, and although he may grumble, he will obey.

How the Phlegmatic Temperament Learns

Learning from Adult Behavior

The melancholic child can develop sympathy for others by observing the compassionate way a parent or teacher handles her own painful experiences. The choleric child needs to feel respect for an authority figure. The sanguine child will learn from an adult with whom he can develop personal love. Imitation, especially imitating adult behavior, is the way the phlegmatic child learns.

Learning by Imitation

Because the phlegmatic temperament lacks imagination, these children can become slaves to patterns of repetition. In working with your child, gently *show* him what to do, knowing that he is well able to imitate and would prefer to copy someone else rather than repeat his own effort. Be careful not to miss any steps in your instruction, or those steps will be missed when he goes to do the assignment. Parents can show their phlegmatic child how to play a new game, or teach him the proper way to fold clothes or set the dinner table, and then help him with each new skill until he can master it on his own.

Sharing Other's Interests

The phlegmatic child needs lots of playmates, as his interests will be awakened through theirs. If friends are interested in dinosaurs, use this as an opportunity to take your child and his friends to the dinosaur exhibit at the museum. If childhood friends are planning a trip to the Grand Canyon, pull out the map and travel books on the Grand Canyon so your phlegmatic child can share the interest and excitement. Parents will want to introduce their child to many children his own age, but be sure to stay with him in unfamiliar situations until he is comfortable.

> *Our friend's mother attempted to expand her phlegmatic child's interests by encouraging her daughter to join a group making dried-flower arrangements for the town's shut-in residents. Although the gesture was well intentioned, it backfired. The child was very uncomfortable among all these strangers doing something she had never done before and didn't know how to do. If her mother had shown her how to make the arrangements first, and then joined her for the first couple of activity sessions to support her and introduce her to all the new people, it would have been a more comfortable experience for her child and could have created a positive outcome.*

Since these children are not self-starters and are happy to live within their quiet and safe comfort zone, parents and teachers can encourage the phlegmatic's participation by involving him in the activity of other children. He will get caught up in the action and momentum as he joins other children in their game or study group.

Learning from Repeatable Tasks

When preparing for a dinner party, you can ask your phlegmatic youngster to set the table. Because the task always includes the same steps, it will be done accurately each time, and he will feel useful and included. Be sure to demonstrate exactly how you want the table set and then your child can repeat it.

Give Them Goals

These children need measurable goals. Be very clear to tell them what you expect of them and by when; "I expect you to have your bed made in twenty minutes" or "I want you to complete ten math problems in forty-five minutes." When the phlegmatic child experiences a sense of accomplishment, which measurable goals help to define, he feels very good about himself. If your child is left to drift without guidance or goals, he will not feel satisfied.

Overcoming Boredom

It is important not to become your phlegmatic child's entertainment director. When your youngster becomes really stuck in an apathetic mood (which will happen from time to time), surround him with things and events for which he should be apathetic. It may seem counterintuitive, but watching a front-load washing machine or dryer go round and round, counting the pennies in the family penny jar, and other "boring" activities are what is called for at these times. The old farmer's saying, "Let's go outside and watch the grass grow," describes what's needed here. The child will *eventually* become bored and will then be ready to find something more stimulating in which to be interested.

AWAKING THE PHLEGMATIC

The phlegmatic can be frustrating for family members because he does not want to take a risk expressing his opinion. He is painfully uncomfortable in the limelight and hates doing anything that will draw attention to him or cause someone to expect something from him. As the phlegmatic evolves, he can grow to enjoy social gatherings as long as he is not expected to make himself conspicuous. This temperament does not have imaginative inventiveness. He is unlikely to take the initiative to get involved in anything that requires energy and passion, such as family disputes, where to go on vacation, home décor, or playground arguments.

Moderate Sleep and Diet

This temperament, more than the other three, loves to sleep. Don't be afraid to wake the child an hour early in the morning and keep him occupied with making his bed, setting the table for breakfast, and getting dressed. In his book *The Temperaments in Education*, Roy Wilkinson observes that the phlegmatic loves to eat and tends to become overweight from lack of physical activity and a generally slow metabolism. Because of his sluggish metabolism, parents are advised not to allow this child to overeat, especially starches.

While waiting to go to school, a phlegmatic child was repeatedly observed slowly unwrapping his lunch, looking longingly at each piece in turn, then happily and slowly wrapping it back up and putting it back into his lunch box. Like Winnie the Pooh, this child is always helpful to his friends, but nothing will get in the way of his afternoon snack!

Awaking His Dreamy Nature

Your child needs personal contact to awaken him to activity. Teachers are encouraged to shock him to awareness by clapping hands or banging on the desk. While the phlegmatic student is momentarily awake, some important message or piece of information can be communicated to him. Efforts made to awaken the phlegmatic while he is a child may obviate the need to "hit him over the head with a two-by-four" when he is an adult.

The Blessing of the Phlegmatic Temperament

Great patience and creativity are needed with phlegmatic children, who can then bring many blessings in adulthood. Knud Asbjorn

Lund makes the point in his book, *Understanding Our Fellow Men*, that the adult phlegmatic will show lifelong gratitude to the person who has somewhere along the way helped him to overcome his shyness, sleepiness, and reserve.

The phlegmatic is like the tortoise in the story of *The Tortoise and the Hare*. He may be very slow out of the gate, but he methodically gets to the finish line first, without emotion and stress, and with adequate savings in the bank. Although the phlegmatic begins by spurning all new experiences, he can learn to absorb the interests of his friends and so widen his small world. And he shows the rest of us how to endure, how to tackle the dull everyday tasks, and how to stay focused to the very end. The phlegmatic is conservative and faithful, upright and honorable, and is an example for us all.

THE PHLEGMATIC ADULT

DEVELOPING EFFECTIVE RELATIONSHIPS

"If you obey all the rules, you miss all the fun."
—**Katherine Hepburn**

THE THREE STAGES OF THE ADULT PHLEGMATIC TEMPERAMENT

The first stage phlegmatic could be described as shy, dull, and uninterested in what goes on about him. When the melancholic grumbles, she is keenly conscious of herself. This is not the case with the phlegmatic. He merely wants to retire into his shell and enjoy the physical pleasure of not letting himself be worried by the outside world. He does not like to be intruded upon, and he dislikes moving too quickly. He relies on what has worked in the past, or what is traditional, rather than being original. Routine is extremely important to him: regular mealtimes and bedtime. He is generally easy-going, but he needs advance warning of changes in his routine to avoid an outburst of ill will. Projects will be completed to the last detail, assuming complete instructions were given at the start. He takes quite a bit of time to do any task, so patience is required by others. Once he learns a process, he retains the information and can be relied upon to complete it correctly each time.

The second-stage phlegmatic vacillates between old comforts and new situations. He is not intuitively social, so he must rely on others to learn how to take an interest in people. It is not unusual for this temperament to neglect to ask someone how they are, but by the second stage he is learning social graces. If a phlegmatic respects someone, he will learn from that person by imitating them, and he will express his gratitude to those who help him overcome his reticence with devotion and loyalty. He will begin to move out into the world and will start to relax at social gatherings as long as he is not pressured to perform. Of course, there is still room for improvement.

The third-stage phlegmatic is like an old shoe, comfortable and reliable. He is sensitive to other people's needs, and his relaxed demeanor is easy to be around. He is well established, grounded, and knowledgeable and is able to teach other people how to do a task well. He has learned to take problems in his stride and keep them at a distance. In social situations he makes a very considerate host, and because he knows about the finer things in life, he enjoys sharing them. He is a trusted member of his family, his community, and society. In her book *Soul Weaving*, Betty Staley describes the phlegmatic as the temperament of old age—a time for acceptance of life. The third-stage phlegmatic enjoys what he can and exudes peace and quiet, order and rhythm.

The Phlegmatic Parent

The phlegmatic parent projects peace and calm into the often chaotic life of children. He is devoted to them and will see to their needs and comfort. The daily routine (regular bedtimes, mealtimes, exercise) will provide a solid basis for a healthy, happy life for the children. The home atmosphere will be orderly and serene, unless an unpleasant surprise produces a temporary storm. The children can depend on this parent to be fair and to do what is promised. Changes will occur only gradually, so the children may need to prepare Mom or Dad to accept the idea of a new bike or prom dress.

- If your child has a *sanguine* temperament, the "regular and unvarying phlegmatic routine" will feel like prison. All children require routine, but the sanguine thrives on surprise and change. The challenge for the phlegmatic parent will be to build variety into the schedule, or to accept last minute surprises (can my friend stay for dinner) with grace. Creating a list of "Expected Behaviors" or "Chores" along with an accompanying list of "Rewards" will help manage the temperament tug-of-war between the routine-loving phlegmatic parent and the "flighty," routine-hating sanguine child. Play dates with other children that include artistic or creative activities will be essential.

- The *phlegmatic* child will be content with the healthy routine of regular meals and bedtimes that the phlegmatic parent will instinctively provide. He will become dull, however, without some distractions in his life, so the phlegmatic parent should plan to organize play dates for him and accompany him when going to new places and meeting new people.

- The phlegmatic parent who is unable to stand up to arguments or challenges to his position or point of view will lose his *choleric* child's respect. As the phlegmatic is uncomfortable in an argumentative environment, therapist Shepha Vainstein (herself a phlegmatic parent) suggests it might be helpful to create a "Privileges" list and a "Bad Behavior" list. When a bad behavior occurs, a privilege is lost. There is no argument, just a reference to the list and the ensuing result. This routine, carried out consistently, will help to ground the choleric child. Although this parent may want to protect his child from the "knock-downs" in life, this is not helpful for .the choleric child because overcoming challenges is how he learns and grows.

- Being introverted and extremely serious, the *melancholic* child will feel unseen and misunderstood by the phlegmatic adult who seems to ignore or downplay the seriousness of her maladies and distress. While too much attention to the melancholic child's stresses will only make her more fearful, working with your child to conduct an *objective* review of her troubles, and adding a hug at the end, is most supportive.

The challenge for the phlegmatic parent: Learn to enjoy the exceptions to the routine that life with children will always manage to supply. Find ways to enjoy getting to know something or someone new with your children. Your challenge will be to show enough interest to really listen to your children so they feel heard and loved.

FINAL THOUGHTS

At the end of a fifteen-year research project, Jerome Kagen wistfully concluded that after taking into consideration variables such as family atmosphere, heredity, physical environment, and ethnicity, an individual's temperament is not impacted by outside factors. In other words, even though a person came from a happy and balanced home life, free from trauma and abnormal stress, if they had a dominant melancholic temperament, he or she would still experience the world as a painful place. Therefore, this scientist concluded in his book *Galen's Prophecy* that he would just have to learn to "accept" people for who they are and give up the hope that something external could "change" them.

We have stressed that our intention in writing *Authentic Parenting* is to give parents concepts and tools for recognizing their child's individual temperament. With an awakened awareness of the four temperaments and how they manifest as personality traits, parents can learn how to accept something that cannot be changed within the child's personality, and learn how to turn what is there into a strength that the child can use. From recognition and acceptance comes understanding and love for the individuality that dwells within the body of the child.

Each temperament provides a special challenge for parents, but it also offers a road map about how to speak to and work with your child. By accepting melancholic children and guiding them to strengthen their sense of compassion for others, parents help create a pathway for this temperament to express itself in positive ways. Plays such as *Death of a Salesman, A Streetcar Named Desire,* and *Long Day's Journey into Night* are by authors who could communicate the depths of the human condition from the perspective of a melancholic temperament. Mother Theresa, whose life mission was to minister to the poorest and most vulnerable human beings, taught the world the real meaning of compassion. It is out of the seriousness of the melancholic temperament that she remained devoted to the sick, hungry, and dying men, women, and children whom she served her entire life.

The choleric temperament can be exceptionally strong-willed and can feel like too much to manage. It will never be possible for this child to sit back and let others be in charge. If adults are willing to work with "what is," this child doesn't need to be labeled as a bully. Parents and teachers can direct the choleric's powerful energy into leadership roles, in the classroom, as well as on the play yard. With conscious guidance, adults can challenge the choleric child to develop self-discipline. After all, it is not possible to lead others until you know how to govern yourself. Qualities that make great leaders (like tenacity, a strong work ethic, self-awareness, and loyalty) are buried in seed form within the young choleric's personality. Like Michelangelo freeing a beautiful sculpture from a piece of marble, parents and teachers can work with choleric children to unfetter them from the temperament's undisciplined personality aspects and guide them to harness and direct their energy toward becoming worthy leaders capable of achieving their goals.

Without parents who understand the nature of the sanguine temperament, these children grow up to be adults who incessantly beat themselves up because they feel like failures. The temperament is stimulated by change and social interaction, and completing any project is truly hard work for them and not very much fun. The parent or teacher who recognizes the shortcomings of sanguine children can help them learn techniques for completing tasks. If such children recognize that they can take on a project and finish it (even with the help of an adult), then mature sanguines will realize that they are capable, responsible human beings. Without conscious guidance, sanguine children will want to do only what they enjoy and will grow into adults who are challenged to buckle down when focus and hard work are needed.

The fields of design and entertainment are filled with successful people who have learned how to capitalize on the strength of their sanguine temperament. This personality will shine in any profession that requires inner flexibility, abundant imagination, frequent change, and plenty of human interaction.

It is far too easy to assume phlegmatic children are "slow" or "cannot keep up." Loving parents and teachers will work consciously with these children to stimulate and engage them in the activities of other children with a wider range of interest and a faster metabolism. Otherwise, this boy or girl will live happily in their comfort zone and never stretch beyond it. Phlegmatic children who are accepted, guided, and challenged by knowledgeable parents and teachers will become adults who are solid citizens, stable parents, and hard-working, dedicated employees. Scientific research, teaching, accounting, and engineering are some of the career choices for the phlegmatic temperament. These are the careful, methodical professionals we want on our team. They don't seek the limelight, but they are the support people we rely on to help us make good decisions to get the job done right.

We have isolated each of the four temperaments to make it easier to recognize the one or two that are dominant in your child. As we mature and achieve greater inner and outer balance, we can recognize when aspects of each of the four temperaments are operating in us. We might begin to notice the times when we are being choleric because our will is powerfully engaged in getting a job done; or other times, when we've elected to read a book and ignore all our other responsibilities, or we've become engrossed in cleaning out our desk, that we are being rather phlegmatic. A familiarity with the four temperaments allows us to not only understand and accept our child, but also other adults, including the most important adult in our life—ourselves.

BIBLIOGRAPHY

The following books, people, and articles were consulted while preparing this book, and many are referenced in the text:

Childs, Gilbert, Dr. *An Imp on Either Shoulder: Working on Our Temperaments.* Stroud, UK: Fire Tree Press, 1995.

———. *Balancing Your Temperament.* London: Sophia Books, 1999.

———. *Understand Your Temperament! A Guide to the Four Temperaments: Choleric, Sanguine, Phlegmatic, Melancholic.* London: Sophia Books, 1995.

Devens, "Mimi. LCSW, Class Teacher, Highland Hall Waldorf School" (unpublished interview), 2012.

Holden, Bonnie. "Class Teacher, San Diego Waldorf School" (unpublished interview), 2012.

Lewis, Mona. "Handwork teacher, Highland Hall Waldorf School" (unpublished interview), 2011.

Lund, Knud Asbjörn. *Understanding Our Fellow Men: The Judgment of Character through Trained Observation.* London: New Knowledge Books, 1971.

Poplawski, Thomas. "Fire, Action, Creative." *Renewal* (spring/summer, vol. 20, 2010): 24–27.

———. "The Melancholic Child: Gifts and Challenges." *Renewal* (fall/winter, vol. 10, 2010): 16–20.

Staley, Betty. *Between Form and Freedom: A Practical Guide for the Teenage Years.* Stroud, UK: Hawthorn Press, 1988.

———. *Soul Weaving: How to Shape Your Destiny and Inspire Your Dreams.* Stroud, UK: Hawthorn Press, 1999.

Steiner, Rudolf. *The Four Temperaments.* Karlsruhe, Jan. 19, 1909. New York: Anthroposophic Press, 1968 (in *Anthroposophy in Everyday Life: Practical Training in Thought; Overcoming Nervousness; Facing Karma; The Four Temperaments.* Hudson, NY: Anthroposophic Press, 1995).

Wilkinson, Roy. *The Temperaments in Education.* Sussex, UK: Wilkinson, 1977.

ABOUT THE AUTHORS

Bari Borsky

Bari's sanguine temperament has taken her on a journey that includes travel through twenty-six countries and four careers. Her interest in the four temperaments began in 1971 when she joined an anthroposophic group that studied the soul and spiritual nature of mankind, and the development of human consciousness. Knowledge of the four temperaments helped members of the group to develop understanding for one another's personality. This allowed for powerful and harmonious collaboration on community development projects.

Along with her partner, Bari created and ran a decorative accessory manufacturing business for seventeen years. After selling the business in 2002, she brought her love for community development, business knowledge, and social skills to Highland Hall Waldorf School as Development Director. In 2010 she joined the Grief Coach Academy, where she is a certified Heartbreak to Happiness grief recovery and life coach. In 2011 Bari started Bari Clarity Coaching. Her mission is to help parents find joy through understanding their children, and to help adults navigate heartbreak by learning how to appreciate and love themselves. More information can be found at www.bariclaritycoaching.com.

Judy Haney

Judy has maintained her interest in philosophy and its practical applications since 1967, when she joined an anthroposophic study group. Spurred on by encouragement from this group, she expanded her horizons with several trips to Europe. Law offices allowed Judy to practice working with choleric temperaments, and her work in the corporate office of a local aerospace company provided an opportunity to use and expand skills requiring her phlegmatic/melancholic mood: creating databases and expense-tracking systems for the company's annual stock grant program, creating reports for the finance and legal departments, and writing a how-to manual for the database users.

Judy and Bari have worked with each other's temperaments for over thirty years. In that time they have gained an understanding and appreciation for all four temperaments, making it possible for them to give temperament workshops in the Los Angeles area and to write this book